The Cat Family
The Hyena Family

PAT MORRIS, AMY-JANE BEER

About This Volume

Welcome to the first volume of *Ultimate Wildlife*. In this volume and volume two we are covering the large carnivores. The cat family and the hyena family are featured in volume one and the dogs and bears in volume two. They all eat flesh, but do not always kill other animals to get it and may instead use the remains of dead animals. Some, such as lions and tigers, can even be dangerous to humans. Others, such as the smaller cats, feed mainly on small animals, fish, or even insects.

These mammals are found on all continents except Antarctica. Many are solitary, but some live in groups and help each other obtain food. Some are active mainly at night, but others hunt during the day. Several species are now in serious danger of extinction. That is because all large animals are less abundant than smaller ones, and also carnivores are less numerous than their prey. That combination means that certain species must always have been rare. Their numbers have been further reduced because of the threat they appear to pose to people and domestic animals. Several species have fine furs that fetch high prices, encouraging commercial hunters and illegal poachers. Consequently, many large carnivores now have extensive legal protection and major conservation projects aimed at preventing their extinction. The continued existence of large carnivores is important. If they can be conserved successfully, their presence automatically helps preserve viable populations of their prey and other species.

Published by Simply Home Entertainment
Bentima House
168–172 Old Street
London EC1V 9BP

For this edition:

Editorial Director:	Lindsey Lowe
Managing Editor:	Deborah Evans
Creative Director:	Jeni Child
Designer:	John Dinsdale
Picture Researcher:	Sophie Mortimer
Production Director:	Alastair Gourlay
Production:	Richard Berry

Printed in China

ISSN 1758-0994

To subscribe to

Ultimate Wildlife

please ring the
order line on:
0844 848 2008

or visit the website at:
www.ultimate-wildlife.com

Quote the product code 370001

Contents

The puma's distribution range stretches the length of America from Canada in the north to Patagonia in the south.

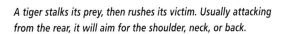

A tiger stalks its prey, then rushes its victim. Usually attacking from the rear, it will aim for the shoulder, neck, or back.

How to Use This Set

*U*ltimate Wildlife is a multi-volume set that describes in detail animals from all corners of the earth. Each volume brings together those animals that are most closely related and have similar lifestyles. For more information on how scientists group animals together and name them, see overleaf. In this series, all the meat-eating mammals (carnivores) are in the first couple of volumes, while other volumes look at, for example, sea mammals (whales and dolphins), or rodents.

Article Styles

You will find three kinds of article in this encyclopedia. There are two types of introductory or overview article: one introduces large animal groups or orders (such as the large carnivores) and the other introduces smaller groups or families (such as hyenas). The articles review the full variety of animals to be found in different groups.

However, the majority of the articles making up each volume concentrates on describing individual animals in great detail. Each article starts with a fact-filled data panel to help you gather information at-a-glance. Used together the different styles of article enable you to become

---

Data panel presents basic statistics of each animal

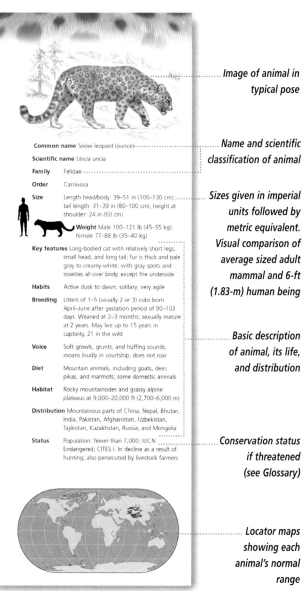

Image of animal in typical pose

Common name Snow leopard (ounce)
Name and scientific classification of animal

Scientific name *Uncia uncia*

Family Felidae

Order Carnivora

Size Length head/body: 39–51 in (100–130 cm); tail length: 31–39 in (80–100 cm); height at shoulder: 24 in (60 cm)
Sizes given in imperial units followed by metric equivalent. Visual comparison of average sized adult mammal and 6-ft (1.83-m) human being

Weight Male 100–121 lb (45–55 kg); female 77–88 lb (35–40 kg)

Key features Long-bodied cat with relatively short legs, small head, and long tail; fur is thick and pale gray to creamy-white, with gray spots and rosettes all over body, except the underside

Habits Active dusk to dawn; solitary; very agile

Breeding Litters of 1–5 (usually 2 or 3) cubs born April–June after gestation period of 90–103 days. Weaned at 2–3 months; sexually mature at 2 years. May live up to 15 years in captivity, 21 in the wild
Basic description of animal, its life, and distribution

Voice Soft growls, grunts, and huffing sounds; moans loudly in courtship; does not roar

Diet Mountain animals, including goats, deer, pikas, and marmots; some domestic animals

Habitat Rocky mountainsides and grassy alpine plateaus at 9,000–20,000 ft (2,700–6,000 m)

Distribution Mountainous parts of China, Nepal, Bhutan, India, Pakistan, Afghanistan, Uzbekistan, Tajikistan, Kazakhstan, Russia, and Mongolia

Status Population: fewer than 7,000; IUCN Endangered; CITES I. In decline as a result of hunting; also persecuted by livestock farmers
Conservation status if threatened (see Glossary)

Locator maps showing each animal's normal range

Article describes a particular animal

Scientific name of animal

Captions to photographs provide additional information about each animal's lifestyle

Common name of animal

LARGE CARNIVORES

Panthera tigris

Tiger

The tiger, with its black-and-orange striped coat, is one of the most distinctive of all mammals. It is feared the world over, but nowadays the species is severely reduced in numbers.

IN MANY WAYS THE TIGER IS MORE deserving of the title King of Beasts than its close cousin, the lion. It is the largest of all the cats, and its range once extended from the fringes of Europe eastward to Russia's Sea of Okhotsk and south to the Indonesian islands of Java and Bali. Tigers from different parts of this vast range differ considerably, so the species are named after the region in which they occur, but most can also be distinguished by their appearance. For example, Siberian tigers are consistently bigger than other subspecies, with males weighing up to 660 pounds (300 kg). This almost certainly makes them the biggest cats ever to have lived, including huge extinct species such as the saber-toothed tiger and the cave lion.

Common name Tiger

Scientific name *Panthera tigris*

Family Carnivora

Order Carnivora

Size Length head/body: 4.6–9 ft (1.4–2.7 m); tail length: 23–43 in (60–110 cm); height at shoulder: 31–43 in (80–110 cm)

Weight Male 200–660 lb (65–165 kg); female 143–364 lb (65–165 kg)

Key features Huge, highly muscular cat with large head and long tail; unmistakable orange coat with dark stripes, underside white

Habits Solitary and highly territorial; active mostly at night; climbs and swims well

Breeding Litters of 1–6 (usually 2 or 3) cubs born at any time of year after gestation period of 95–110 days. Weaned at 3–6 months; females sexually mature at 3–4 years, males at 4–5 years. May live up to 26 years in captivity, rarely more than 10 in the wild

Voice Purrs, grunts, and blood-curdling roars

Diet Mainly large, hooved mammals, including deer, buffalo, antelope, and gaur

Habitat Tropical forests and swamps, grasslands with good vegetation cover and water nearby

Distribution India, Bhutan, Bangladesh, Nepal, China, southeastern Siberia, Myanmar (Burma), Vietnam, Laos, Thailand, and Sumatra

Status Population: 5,000–7,500; IUCN Endangered; CITES I. Previously hunted for fur and body parts, and to protect people and livestock

A Bengal tiger wades through water. Tigers are proficient swimmers and can cross rivers that are 4 to 5 miles (7 to 8 km) wide without difficulty.

Juvenile tiger fond of play fighting like the two below

Different Adaptations

The smallest tigers came from Bali and rarely exceeded 220 pounds (100 kg) in weight. They are now probably extinct. As a general rule, body size relates to the climate and the type of prey available in different parts of the tiger's range. Siberian tigers need to cope with intensely cold and snowy winters, and specialize in catching large prey such as cattle and deer. In contrast, tigers in Indonesia inhabit tropical jungle where overheating is a serious problem for large animals, and the favored prey includes pigs and small deer. The Chinese tiger is thought to be the ancestor of the other types. Fossils show that tigers first appeared in China about 2 million years ago, and they spread north, south, and west from there. Modern Chinese tigers have several traits that zoologists consider rather primitive, including a shortened skull and relatively close-set eyes.

Easy-to-read and comprehensive text

---

familiar with specific animals in the context of their evolutionary history and biological relationships.

A number of other features presents you with helpful extra information. In each volume you will find a detailed list of the species within each family covered in the volume. You will also find a **Glossary** that will help you if there are words in the text that you do not fully understand. Each volume includes a list of useful **Websites** that help you take your research further.

Who's Who tables summarize classification of each major group ....

Introductory article describes major groups of animals

SMALL CARNIVORES

Graphic full-color photographs bring text to life

At-a-glance boxes cover topics of special interest

The Disappearing Tiger

Detailed maps clarify points described in text

Meticulous drawings illustrate a typical selection of group members

Introductory article describes family or closely related groups

THE HYENA FAMILY

The Hyena Family

Tables summarize classification of groups and give examples of animals in the groups. They also list the total number of genera and species in each group

5

Animal Families

*U*ltimate Wildlife – The Cat Family and the Hyena *Family* is the first part of a multi-volume set. Each volume features species that are grouped together because they share similar characteristics. The first volumes are about mammals, and this particular volume focuses on the cats and hyenas. The volumes are arranged to collect together the animals in the categories that are recognized by scientists.

The Animal Kingdom

The living world is divided into five kingdoms, and animals (Animalia) make up one of those kingdoms.

The other kingdoms are Plantae (plants), Fungi, Protista (single-celled life-forms, including algae) and Monera (which includes bacteria). The animal kingdom is divided into numerous major groups called phyla, but only one of them (Chordata) contains those animals that have a backbone. Chordates, or vertebrates, as they are popularly known, include all the animals familiar to us and those most studied by scientists – mammals, birds, fish, reptiles, and amphibians. In all, there are at least 38,000 species of vertebrates, while the phyla that contain animals without backbones (invertebrates, such as insects and spiders) include several million species, probably many more.

Mammals in particular

The volumes on mammals focus on the most familiar of animals, those most easily recognized as having fur (although this may be absent in many sea mammals, like whales and dolphins) and that provide milk for their young. Mammals are divided into major groups (carnivores, primates, rodents, and marsupials, to name just a few). All the major groups are shown on the diagram, left. So, for example, you can see that

Carnivores (Order Carnivora): raccoons, weasels, otters, skunks, cats, dogs, bears, hyenas, seals, sea lions

Pangolins (Order Pholidota)

Odd-toed ungulates (Order Perissodactyla): horses, rhinoceroses, tapirs

Whales, dolphins, and Even-toed Ungulates (Order Cetartiodactyla)

Bats (Order Chiroptera)

Insectivores (Order Eulipotyphla): shrews, moles, hedgehogs

Primates (Order Primates): lemurs, monkeys, apes (and humans)

Lagomorphs (Order Lagormorpha): rabbits, hares, pikas

Rodents (Order Rodentia): squirrels, rats, mice, cavies, porcupines

Colugos, Flying lemurs (Order Dermoptera)

Tree shrews (Order Scandentia)

Xenarthrans (Orders Pilosa and Cingulata): anteaters, sloths, armadillos

Hyraxes (Order Hyracoidea)

Elephants (Order Proboscidea)

Dugongs, manatees (Order Sirenia)

Aardvark (Order Tubulidentata)

Sengis (Order Macroscelidea)

Tenrecs and Golden moles (Order Afrosoricida)

Marsupials (Supercohort: Marsupialia, contains several Orders): opossums, kangaroos, koala

Monotremes (Order Monotremata): platypus, echidnas

The chart shows the major groups of mammals, arranged in evolutionary relationship.

| 200 | 145 | 65 | 55 | 34 | 24 | 5 | 1.8 |

million years ago

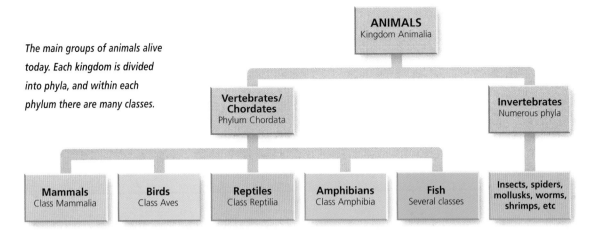

The main groups of animals alive today. Each kingdom is divided into phyla, and within each phylum there are many classes.

ANIMALS
Kingdom Animalia

Vertebrates/Chordates
Phylum Chordata

Invertebrates
Numerous phyla

Mammals
Class Mammalia

Birds
Class Aves

Reptiles
Class Reptilia

Amphibians
Class Amphibia

Fish
Several classes

Insects, spiders, mollusks, worms, shrimps, etc

seals and sea lions followed a very similar evolution to the carnivores until relatively recently (in evolutionary terms).

Naming Mammals

To be able to discuss animals, names are needed for the different kinds. Most people regard tigers as one kind of animal and lions as another. All tigers look more or less alike. They breed together and produce young like themselves. This popular distinction between kinds of animals corresponds closely to the zoologists' distinction between species. All tigers belong to one species and all lions to another. The lion species has different names in different languages (for example, *Löwe* in German, *Simba* in Swahili), and often a single species may have several common names. For example, the North American mountian lion is also known as the cougar, puma, panther, and catamount.

Zoologists find it convenient to have internationally recognized names for species and use a standardized system of two-word Latin names. The lion is called *Panthera leo* and the tiger *Panthera tigris*. The first word, *Panthera*, is the name of the genus (a group of closely similar species), which includes the lion and the tiger. The second word, *leo* or *tigris*, indicates the particular species within the genus. Scientific names are recognized all over the world. The scientific name is used whatever the language, even when the alphabet is different, as in Chinese or Russian. The convention allows for precision and helps avoid most confusion. However, it is also common for one species to apparently have more that one scientific name. That can be because a particular species may have been described and named at different times without the zoologists knowing it was one species.

It is often necessary to make statements about larger groups of animals: for example, all the catlike animals or all the mammals. A formal system of classification makes this possible. Domestic cats are similar to lions and tigers, but not as similar as those species are to each other (for example, they do not roar). They are put in a different genus (*Felis*), but *Felis*, *Panthera*, and other catlike animals are all grouped together as the family Felidae. The flesh-eating mammals (cats, dogs, hyenas, weasels, and so on), together with a few plant-eaters that are obviously related to them (such as pandas), are grouped in the order Carnivora. These and all the other animals that suckle their young are grouped in the class Mammalia. Finally, the mammals are included, with all other animals that have backbones (fish, amphibians, reptiles, and birds) and some other animals that seem to be related to them, in the phylum Chordata.

Rank	Scientific name	Common name
Phylum	Chordata	Animals with a backbone
Class	Mammalia	All mammals
Order	Carnivora	Flesh-eaters/carnivores
Family	Felidae	All cats
Genus	*Panthera*	Big cats
Species	*leo*	Lion

The kingdom Animalia is subdivided into groups such as classes, families, genera, and species. Above is the classification of the lion.

LARGE CARNIVORES

The animals in the first three volumes of this collection are all members of the group Carnivora. The group includes some of the world's biggest and most exciting predators: the tiger, polar bear, and gray wolf, for example. The families of larger carnivores (meat-eating animals) have been grouped together in the first two volumes because they are generally larger than other carnivores . However, that is not to say that some members of the group are not rather small. The bobcat, for example, is much smaller than the European badger or the giant otter. But as a close relative of a giant like the tiger, it qualifies as a large carnivore.

Origins

Fossil records show that many of the largest animals that ever lived are now extinct. During the Miocene and Pleistocene periods (26 to 2 million years ago) there was a general tendency toward the development of giant species, many of which are now legendary—the woolly mammoth or Irish elk, for example. The carnivores were no exception and once included such formidable beasts as the saber-toothed tiger and the cave bear. However, the largest carnivores that ever lived are still with us—the tiger and polar bear are the largest-ever members of the cat and bear families respectively.

Characteristics

Along with the small carnivores in Volume 3 all these animals have the characteristic carnivore dentition, including long canine teeth and molar teeth with pointed cusps (knobs) on their surface. Four of the largest molars, called the carnassials, are specialized for cutting meat rather than crushing it. However, the larger members of the order Carnivora are less carnivorous than their smaller cousins, and many eat large quantities of plant material. Some, such as the giant panda, are almost exclusively vegetarian. Most bears are omnivores, and many do not have the distinctive carnassials used by meat eaters to cut meat and tough skin.

Among those species that hunt and kill other animals for food, hunting techniques include solitary stalk-and-pounce attacks (most cats), ambush (leopard), wonderful examples of teamwork (lions, African wild dogs), short, fast chases (cheetah), and long, drawn-out pursuits over

several miles (wolf). Being large means that many of these animals are able to tackle large prey, and there are few land-dwelling mammals that are not preyed on by at least one large carnivore.

Most large carnivores live solitary lives except when courting and rearing a family, but there are exceptions. In fact, the large carnivores include some of the world's most sociable mammals. Carnivores that live in groups can be models of well-ordered society (such as lions and wolves) or uneasy coalitions of animals drawn together by a clustered food source or the need for security in numbers (brown bears and spotted hyenas, for example).

Most large carnivores are digitigrade, meaning that they have small, neat feet and walk on their toes. Only the bears walk on the whole foot (plantigrade) and appear rather flat-footed and clumsy as a result.

Despite their bulk, large carnivores are often remarkably nimble. Most can run fast, climb well, and several are excellent swimmers. The clouded leopard is acrobatic enough to be able to dangle by one foot from a tree in order to swipe at small prey, and the huge polar bear can sneak across thin ice that would not support a man, using its huge flat feet to disperse the effect of its enormous weight.

⊖ *A family of cheetahs on the African plains.*
Cheetahs can run faster than any other animal,
mainly because their spines are extremely flexible.

Carnivores and Humans

Large carnivores need abundant prey to provide them with enough to eat and must always live well spaced out to avoid consuming all the food available in one place. Therefore they are naturally scarce. That makes them vulnerable when hunting pressures or loss of habitat cause further reductions in numbers. The animals soon become too spaced out to maintain their population, and extinction follows. That is why many larger carnivores are now officially listed as threatened species by the IUCN.

The large carnivores have been traditionally hated by humans because of their predatory habits. Carnivores have been trapped, shot, poisoned, and killed in their dens for centuries. As a result, some are teetering on the brink of extinction, while others have already disappeared. At the other end of the scale two species in particular owe not only their huge success but also their very existence to humans: The domestic dog and cat are the most widespread and numerous large carnivores on earth.

9

The Cat Family

Cats are perhaps the ultimate carnivores. They are swift runners, agile climbers, and can jump and swim well. Different species specialize in one or two forms of locomotion in order to hunt their preferred prey more efficiently. Cats have short, rounded heads, lithe, muscular bodies, and are deep chested to accommodate large lungs. They also have long legs ending in five toes on the forefeet and four on the back. Except for the cheetah, all cats have very sharp, hooked claws that retract into fleshy sheaths to prevent them from becoming chipped or blunted. The cheetah—the most ancient type of cat alive today—has underdeveloped claws that cannot retract.

What Is a Cat?

In terms of anatomy cats are all very similar: Take away the skin, and it would be difficult to tell most species apart other than by size. This varies considerably from the tiny 13–20 inch (34–50 cm) long, 3.3–6 pound (1.5–2.7 kg)

black-footed cat (*Felis nigripes*) to the largest tigers, which can be 9 feet (2.8 m) long and weigh over 660 pounds (300 kg). The earliest cats appeared about 50 million years ago in the Eocene period. They were quite small, but by the Oligocene period (30 million years ago) the family was dominated by huge saber-toothed cats, such as the infamous *Smilodon fatalis*. This awesome animal was the size of a modern lion, with greatly elongated upper canine teeth. It could not bite hard or chew; indeed, the jaws were not particularly strong. All the power came from huge neck muscles, which enabled the cat to open its mouth cavernously wide and use its teeth like daggers, slashing and stabbing at the arteries in the prey's throat.

Saber-toothed cats were the dominant mammalian predators on earth until about 2 million years ago. They died out as recently as the last ice age, 10,000 years ago, and would certainly have been around during the Stone Age, when they must have been a terrifying prospect for humans living at the time.

Well Balanced

Cats have an ability to land on their feet. Even in free fall they sense which way is up and rapidly twist their heads into an upright position. Most cats have a long tail, which they use to help their balance when running and climbing. Usually the tail is carried in a downward curve, but some cats occasionally hold theirs upright. In many species the tip of the tail is black, which probably helps make it more visible to young when they are following their mother.

Cats have large, forward-facing eyes and good eyesight. A layer of reflective material behind the retina at the back of the eye (called the *tapetum lucidum*) helps direct as much available light as possible onto the retina, improving visual sensitivity and giving cats their excellent

⊕ *The caracal, a small cat from Africa and the Near East, is distinguished by large, tufted ears and a slender face. Caracals are agile hunters that, like servals, make acrobatic leaps into the air to catch prey.*

Family Felidae: 12 genera, 38 species	
Acinonyx	1 species, cheetah (*A. jubatus*)
Panthera	4 species, lion (*P. leo*); tiger (*P. tigris*); leopard (*P. pardus*); jaguar (*P. onca*)
Felis	6 species, including domestic cat (*F. catus*); Chinese desert cat (*F. bieti*); wildcat (*F. silvestris*); black-footed cat (*F. nigripes*); sand cat (*F. margarita*); jungle cat (*F. chaus*)
Neofelis	2 species, clouded leopards (*N. nebulosa* and *N. diardi*)
Caracal	3 species, caracal (*C. caracal*); African golden cat (*C. aurata*); Serval (*C. serval*)
Leopardus	7 species, ocelot (*L. pardalis*); pampas cat (*L. colocolo*); kodkod (*L. guigna*); Geoffroy's cat (*L. geoffroyi*); mountain cat (*L. jabobita*); tiger cat (*L. triginus*); margay cat (*L. wiedii*)
Lynx	4 species, lynx (*L. lynx*); Canadian lynx (*L. canadensis*); Iberian lynx (*L. pardinus*); bobcat (*L. rufus*)
Otocolobus	1 species, Pallas's cat (*O. manul*)
Pardofelis	3 species, bay cat (*P. badia*); Marbled cat (*P. marmorata*); Asiatic golden cat (*P. temminck*)
Prionailurus	4 species, lynx (*L. lynx*); Canadian lynx (*L. canadensis*); Iberian lynx (*L. pardinus*); bobcat (*L. rufus*)
Puma	2 species, puma (*P. concolor*), jaguarundi (*P. yaguarondo*
Uncia	1 species, snow leopard (*U. unica*)

night vision. This layer is what makes a cat's eyes appear to glow in the dark when caught by a bright light such as a car headlight. The long-held mystical reputation of cats may be partly explained by their "eyeshine." In fact, the word "lynx" comes from the Greek, meaning "to shine."

Night Stalkers

Most cats are active at night, some exclusively so, and their sensitive whiskers provide a useful backup to vision. The length of the whiskers is related to the size of the cat. If a cat can push its head into a space without its whiskers touching the sides, it can proceed with confidence, knowing that the rest of its body will follow without getting jammed. Cats also have excellent hearing, and many are able to pinpoint prey using their large ears to focus on small, directional sounds. Compared with dogs, cats do not have a well-developed sense of smell.

Nevertheless, scent is still important as a means of communication, especially among the more territorial species, such as tigers and jaguars. All cats use urine, feces, and scratches to mark out their territory. Like a number of other mammals, cats have an extrasensory organ in the mouth, called Jacobson's organ. This enables cats to detect chemicals in the air, particularly sex pheromones (a chemical substance produced by an animal in order to stimulate others of the same species).

⊕ *Ten species of small cat, shown left to right, reflecting their west (America) to east (Asia) distribution: ocelot (1); tiger cat (2); jaguarundi (3); European wildcat (4); African wildcat (5); black-footed cat (6); sand cat (7); jungle cat (8); leopard cat (9); Asiatic golden cat (10). The range of the cat family is extensive and includes all continents except Antarctica and Australasia.*

Domestic Cats

The domestic cat has been honed by centuries of selective breeding into about 30 recognized breeds. While there is fossil evidence of African wildcats living alongside humans as long as 7,000 years ago, it was not until 4,000 years ago that domestic cats became distinguishable from wild ones. Even now the distinction is hazy, since true wild and feral (gone wild) cats interbreed readily.

In ancient Egypt cats were revered as gods. Thousands of mummified cats have been discovered entombed alongside the Pharaohs, and one entire city, known as Bubastis, appears to have been built in their honor by a cult of cat worshippers.

A bronze sculpture of an Egyptian cat dating from the Saite dynasty (about 600 BC).

A Coat of Many Colors

Cats have highly variable coats, including some that are lustrous and spectacularly beautiful. The fur can be short and sleek or deep and fluffy. The background color varies from white to black and includes all shades of gray, buff, yellow, orange, red, and brown. The coat can be plain or marked with spots, blotches, stripes, rosettes, and streaks. Each one is as unique as a fingerprint, so individual cats can often be told apart by their coat patterns. The function of the patterns is usually to break up the cat's outline, making it difficult to see in its favored habitat.

For some cats their superb coat has attracted unwelcome human attention, and many species have a long history of hunting by humans. The fashion for cat fur peaked in the 1960s, when hundreds of thousands of cats, especially big spotted ones, such as leopards, ocelots, and jaguars, were killed for their coats. Some

1

2

3

4

5

pelts could fetch several hundred dollars apiece. Consequently, many species are now rare or extinct in large parts of their former range.

Where Cats Live

The natural range of the cat family is extensive, including all continents except Antarctica and Australasia. Until the introduction of domestic animals all over the world, cats were absent from most islands. Cats occupy all kinds of habitats from dense jungle or coniferous forest to tropical grassland, tundra, deserts, and mountains. Some cats, such as the snow leopard, are highly adapted to a particular niche. Others are true generalists: In fact, the leopard, puma, and wildcat are among the most widespread of all mammals.

Lifestyle

Except for courting pairs and mothers with offspring, most cats are solitary animals. In some species home ranges may overlap extensively, but the occupants are still at pains to avoid each other. Other species are highly territorial, and intruders are met with outright hostility. However, some cats—especially lions—are more tolerant of company and live in prides of related animals.

The size of a cat's home range is less important than the content. Solitary cats, in particular, need a safe den in which to rear their family. A single cat may have several dens or favorite hiding places within its range, and they can include caves, hollow trees, and thickets of dense vegetation. The other vital requirement is an adequate supply of prey. Prey species range from huge wild cattle to the tiniest mouse or even beetles.

Hunting techniques vary surprisingly little, and almost all are based on stalk and dash or sometimes an ambush, followed

⊕ *A pride of lions in the Serengeti National Park, northern Tanzania (Africa). Lions are by far the most social of the cats. The pride is the unit of social life and usually consists of three to 10 adult females, their offspring, and a coalition of two to three adult males. Some prides have been known to contain as many as 18 adult females and 10 adult males.*

by a leap or pounce that knocks the prey over or pins it down. Vertebrate prey is usually killed with a bite to the neck or a stranglehold on the throat. Solitary cats that kill large animals often go to great lengths to hide their half-eaten prey so they can return to feed over several days. For social species, like the lion, teamwork raises the kill rate and allows some adult members of the pride the luxury of not having to catch their own food.

Young cats are born blind and helpless, and rely entirely on their mothers for an extended period. Weaning can begin quite early, but it is months or even years before the kittens can fend for themselves.

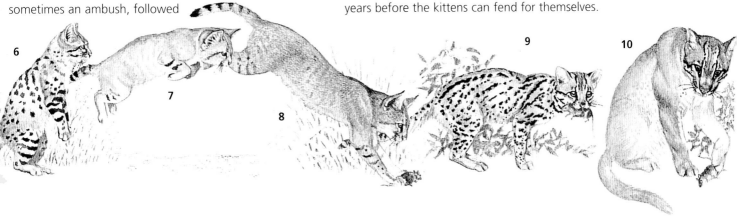

6

7

8

9

10

Common name Lion

Scientific name *Panthera leo*

Family	Felidae
Order	Carnivora
Size	Length head/body: 5–8 ft (1.4–2.5 m); tail length: 27.5–41 in (70–105 cm); height at shoulder: 42–48 in (107–123 cm). Male 20–50% bigger than female

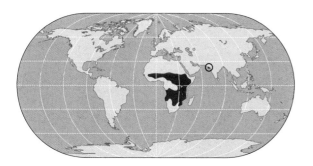

Weight 265–550 lb (120–250 kg)

Key features	Huge, muscular cat with long, thin tail tipped with black tuft; body light buff to tawny brown; male develops thick mane of dark fur; head large with powerful, crushing jaws; eyes yellowish-brown
Habits	Lives in prides; hunts alone and cooperatively; most active between dusk and dawn; rests up to 21 hours per day
Breeding	One to 6 cubs (average 3–4) born after gestation period of 100–119 days. Weaned at 6–7 months; sexually mature at 3–4 years. May live up to 30 years in captivity, rarely more than 13 in the wild
Voice	Variety of puffs, grunts, snarls, and roars
Diet	Large mammal prey, including antelope, giraffe, zebra, hogs, and buffalo; also carrion
Habitat	Savanna grasslands, open woodlands, desert margins, and scrub
Distribution	Scattered populations in sub-Saharan Africa; population in Gir Forest, northwestern India
Status	Population: several thousand; IUCN Vulnerable; CITES II. Asian lions fewer than 300; IUCN Endangered; CITES I. Declining outside protected areas

Lion

Panthera leo

Lions are by far the most social of the cats, breeding and hunting in large family groups. The male, with his magnificent mane, is much larger than the female, but lionesses are the superior hunters.

THE LION HAS ALWAYS BEEN REGARDED with awe. It is enshrined in the myths and legends of many cultures, and its popular image as the King of Beasts goes back to ancient times.

Widespread

Fossil evidence and cave paintings show that lions were once among the world's most widespread land-dwelling animals, second only to humans. During the Pleistocene era (2 million to 10,000 years ago) there were lions not only in Africa but throughout Eurasia and the Americas. The American and northern European varieties went extinct after the last ice age as forests grew up and human hunters advanced, depleting stocks of the lion's main prey. In southern Europe and the Middle East lions lasted a lot longer. The Greek scholar and philosopher Aristotle wrote about lions in 300 BC, and the Romans made grisly sport of pitting the animals against Christians condemned to death. Such lions were captured in North Africa, but the species is now extinct there. Lions were relatively common in the Middle East 500 years ago, and some survived there until as recently as the early 1900s.

Lions have been killed for a variety of reasons, including sport and self-defense. They are not instinctive man-eaters, but they will resort to attacking livestock and people if the availability of natural prey such as deer or antelope is reduced. Lions can become a serious threat to people involved in farming or other activities that bring humans into lion country. One pair of lions reportedly killed and ate 124 people in Uganda in 1925. The victims were

⬆ *Lionesses and cubs keep a close watch on a resting rhinoceros. A rhinoceros can defend itself with the use of its deadly horns, and the lionesses are cautious of approaching.*

Asian Lions

An Asian lion and lioness. Asian lions belong to a separate subspecies from African lions.

The only wild lions living outside Africa today survive in the Gir Forest, a tiny pocket of protected land in northwestern India. They belong to a distinctive and highly threatened subspecies, *Panthera leo persica*, known as the Asian lion.

Asian lions differ from their African cousins in that the males have a much shorter mane, which does not cover the ears or chest. Both sexes have a fold of skin running lengthwise along the belly.

The decline of the Asian lion was largely a result of persecution by humans. In the days of the British Raj shooting lions was a popular pastime. Marksmen showed their hunting prowess by making hundreds of kills. The population dropped to an all-time low of fewer than 100 animals at the start of the 20th century, by which time the Asian lion had been declared a protected animal.

There are currently 120 or so Asian lions living in captivity around the world. While there may be enough to prevent their extinction, the future of Asian lions in the wild is far from secure. The Gir Forest Reserve is now too small for the 250 or so lions that live there. In times of prey shortage they resort to attacking livestock; some have even become man-eaters. Between 1988 and 1991 Gir lions killed 20 people. It is not surprising that suggestions to release some to other reserves in India have met with stiff opposition.

working on the construction of a new railway, a project that eventually had to be abandoned. Today in Africa humans and lions get along much better because most lions now live in large conservation areas such as the great national parks of Kenya, Tanzania, and southern Africa. Here they have the space and prey they need to survive without attacking people, and they contribute to the local economy by attracting fee-paying tourists.

About 20 percent of African lions are nomadic. They live in small groups, the members of which come and go. They wander over a huge area, following migratory herds of antelope and zebra. Nomadic lions are nonterritorial, and most encounters are nonaggressive. However, most lions live in resident prides, jealously guarding the same territory for generations.

Boundary Patrol

Defense of the territory is usually done by the males, but the whole pride helps define the boundaries by roaring, scent marking with urine, and regular patrolling. The size of a pride's home range varies considerably,

⊕ The roar of a lion can be heard over distances of up to 5 miles (8 km) and is used to define boundaries and warn off rivals. Lions also roar after devouring a kill.

Vocal Communication

Lions have a varied repertoire of vocalizations. The various sounds are distinctive and are usually accompanied by body language that makes their meaning obvious, even to humans. Members of a pride use a gentle huffing sound to greet and reassure each other, while purring communicates contentment (for example, when being groomed). Mewing sounds are used mostly by cubs and vary from short squeaks of excitement to yowls of distress. Growls and snarls are warning sounds, while charging lions often give a gruff coughing sound. A "woofing" grunt signifies surprise and is often followed by a sharp hissing or spitting to show displeasure. The best-known lion vocalization is, of course, the roar. Males start roaring from the age of one year, females slightly later. A full-blown roar can easily be heard up to 5 miles (8 km) away, and the sound is used to define territorial boundaries and to intimidate rivals. Roaring in chorus enhances the bonds between pride members. Most roaring happens at night.

depending on the number of animals in the pride and the local abundance of prey. If food is scarce for part of the year, a pride will range over a much larger area. The ranges of neighboring prides may overlap to an extent, but individual lions usually take care to avoid each other. An intruder in the core part of a pride's range will be driven off ferociously.

The need to defend a territory is the main reason why male lions are so much larger than females, up to half as big again in some cases. They need to be big to chase off rivals. Two competing males will size each other up before fighting, and the inferior male will usually back down and go away without a fight. This reduces the risk of these big and well-equipped animals fatally wounding each other. However, there is a definite home advantage; the resident males are more confident and quicker to launch an attack, so they usually win any contest.

The mane is an important factor in male aggression. For a start, a male with a huge mane may be able to fool opponents into believing that he is more powerful than he actually is. If the bluff does not work and a fight ensues, the mane helps protect the vulnerable area around the neck and throat from slashing claws and teeth. The now extinct Barbary lion, a subspecies that lived in North Africa until 1920, had a huge mane that extended well down its back and under its belly.

Female Hunters

The adult male members of a pride do little hunting. Males are capable of catching their own food, but they are rarely as good at it as the females. A large male with a bulky mane will find it difficult to remain inconspicuous, while a slim lioness can creep forward with her body pressed flat to the ground, making use of even very sparse cover. The chances of making

⊕ *A lioness with her cubs. The boisterous rough-and-tumble games of the cubs are tolerated by all members of the pride, since everybody is closely related. Cubs are even allowed to suckle from any female in the group. At less than a year the young cubs will join the lionesses in the hunt, but they are usually more of a hindrance than a help!*

Social Creatures

Lions are by far the most social of the cats. While some individuals live alone, a solitary lifestyle is the exception rather than the rule and loners are usually old males that have been ousted from a pride. Such animals rarely live long.

Lion prides are based on a group of related females, including sisters, daughters, mothers, and grandmothers, most of whom stay with the pride throughout their lives. Females will only be required to leave if the pride gets too big. In such cases small groups splinter off and try to start their own pride. The adult males of the pride are not permanent. In fact, they rarely last more than three or four years before they are displaced by younger, stronger animals. Young males are forced to leave the pride in which they were born at about the time they reach puberty (two to three years of age).

Males often team up to defend a pride. Such coalitions almost always consist of related males (brothers or cousins). On taking over a pride, by killing or driving out the previous males, the first priority is getting the females pregnant. Because female lions cannot breed while they are still suckling young cubs, the males usually kill any cubs younger than about 24 months. Older cubs (especially females approaching breeding age) may escape with their lives, but young males are rarely permitted to remain. The pride females are more inclined to defend older cubs in which they have invested a great deal of care; but on the whole they seem to accept the loss of their cubs and a new boss, and get on with raising a new family.

A receptive female may mate 50 or more times in 24 hours, usually, but not always, with the same male. When the cubs arrive three or four months later, they are usually allowed to suckle from any female, and their boisterous games are tolerated and even encouraged by all members of the pride. This extraordinary benevolence stems from the fact that the members of the pride are closely related. An adult male cannot be sure that the cubs are his offspring, but most will carry his genes and be worth nurturing.

a kill increase when lionesses hunt together. They are highly organized, with different lionesses taking on specialized roles. One female usually takes the lead, selecting the target and signaling the start of the hunt. The fastest females do the chasing, while others ambush and disable the prey. Sometimes the whole pride will join in, fanning out and surrounding the victim. Excitable young cubs are often of little help, but by the age of one year they can make a useful contribution.

Surprise Attack

The lion's hunting technique is all about stealth and surprise. It can run up to 38 miles per hour (60 km/h), but only for short distances. To catch a fleet-footed target such as an impala or zebra, lions need to be within 50 yards (46 m) before launching an attack. They do not usually jump on top of their prey. Instead, they try to knock it off balance with a mighty swipe of the front feet aimed at the prey's flank or rump. Once the prey has been pulled down, the lion clamps its mouth over the throat or muzzle, killing by strangulation or suffocation. The lion can breathe deeply through its nose, so it can keep a tight hold of the prey for as long as necessary, even after a hard chase.

Scavengers

Only about a quarter of hunts are successful, and lions also feed by scavenging. In fact, for some prides four out of five meals are stolen from hyenas, a statistic that contradicts the long-held belief that hyenas routinely harass lions and scavenge their kills. It is actually the opportunist lions that use their superior size and strength to drive the hyenas away.

If the carcass is large, the pride will share the food fairly amicably. On smaller kills there is a definite order of seniority. The males feed first, and young cubs go last. If food is scarce, the cubs are the first to starve.

An adult lion needs to eat an average of 11 to 15 pounds (5 to 7 kg) of meat a day. Males get a good share of a kill, even if they have not participated in the hunt.

Common name Tiger

Scientific name *Panthera tigris*

Family	Felidae
Order	Carnivora
Size	Length head/body: 4.6–9 ft (1.4–2.7 m); tail length: 23–43 in (60–110 cm); height at shoulder: 31–43 in (80–110 cm)
	Weight Male 200–660 lb (90–300 kg); female 143–364 lb (65–165 kg)
Key features	Huge, highly muscular cat with large head and long tail; unmistakable orange coat with dark stripes; underside white
Habits	Solitary and highly territorial; active mostly at night; climbs and swims well
Breeding	Litters of 1–6 (usually 2 or 3) cubs born at any time of year after gestation period of 95–110 days. Weaned at 3–6 months; females sexually mature at 3–4 years, males at 4–5 years. May live up to 26 years in captivity, rarely more than 10 in the wild
Voice	Purrs, grunts, and blood-curdling roars
Diet	Mainly large, hooved mammals, including deer, buffalo, antelope, and gaur
Habitat	Tropical forests and swamps; grasslands with good vegetation cover and water nearby
Distribution	India, Bhutan, Bangladesh, Nepal; China; southeastern Siberia; Myanmar (Burma), Vietnam, Laos, Thailand, and Sumatra
Status	Population: 5,000–7,500; IUCN Endangered; CITES I. Previously hunted for fur and body parts, and to protect people and livestock

Tiger

Panthera tigris

The tiger, with its black-and-orange striped coat, is one of the most distinctive of all mammals. It is feared the world over, but nowadays the species is severely reduced in numbers.

IN MANY WAYS THE TIGER IS MORE deserving of the title King of Beasts than its close cousin, the lion. It is the largest of all the cats, and its range once extended from the fringes of Europe eastward to Russia's Sea of Okhotsk and south to the Indonesian islands of Java and Bali. Tigers from different parts of this vast range differ considerably, so the species has been divided into eight subspecies. They are named after the region in which they occur, but most can also be distinguished by their appearance. For example, Siberian tigers are consistently bigger than other subspecies, with males weighing up to 660 pounds (300 kg). This almost certainly makes them the biggest cats ever to have lived, including huge extinct species such as the saber-toothed tiger and the cave lion.

Different Adaptations

The smallest tigers came from Bali and rarely exceeded 220 pounds (100 kg) in weight. They are now probably extinct. As a general rule, body size relates to the climate and the type of prey available in different parts of the tiger's range. Siberian tigers need to cope with intensely cold and snowy winters, and specialize in catching large prey such as cattle and deer. In contrast, tigers in Indonesia inhabit tropical jungle where overheating is a serious problem for large animals, and the favored prey includes pigs and small deer. The Chinese tiger is thought to be the ancestor of the other types. Fossils show that tigers first appeared in China about 2 million years ago, and they spread north, south, and west from there. Modern Chinese tigers have several traits that zoologists consider rather primitive, including a shortened skull and relatively close-set eyes.

↱ *A Bengal tiger wades through water. Tigers are proficient swimmers and can cross rivers that are 4 to 5 miles (7 to 8 km) wide without difficulty.*

↴ *Juvenile tigers are fond of play fighting, like the two below.*

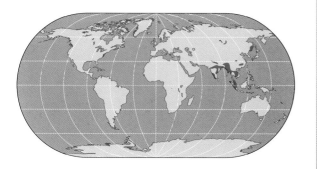

The Disappearing Tiger

Subtle differences aside, all tigers have the same adaptations to a predatory way of life. They have long hind limbs that enable them to cover up to 30 feet (10 m) in a single bound. Their forelegs are immensely powerful and armed with long claws that can be retracted when the tiger is walking. The tiger uses this combination to deadly effect when hunting. It usually rushes prey from behind, either knocking it to the ground with the force of its charge or hooking its claws into the rump or flank and dragging the animal over. Smaller prey is dispatched with a bite to the neck. The tiger's canine teeth are long, sharp, and slightly

The decline in range and numbers of the magnificent tiger is well documented. Logging and the expansion of agriculture have removed huge areas of tiger habitat. Hunting has also reduced tiger numbers substantially. Of the eight recognized subspecies of tiger the Caspian, Bali, and Javan tigers have become extinct in the last 50 years. Siberian and Chinese tigers are listed by the IUCN as Critically Endangered, and the Sumatran, Indochinese, and Bengal tigers are listed as Endangered.

All tigers are supposed to be protected by international law, but even in some national parks and reserves illegal hunting continues. The biggest threat is the demand for tiger body parts for use in traditional Asian medicine. In the past the main culprits were the Chinese, who have hunted their own wild tigers to virtual extinction. Today tigers are hunted by poachers everywhere. Body parts are then smuggled into China, where they are turned into pills and potions, many of which are exported and sold on the black market for vast sums. Some, such as ground bone to treat rheumatism, can be bought in Asian communities the world over. Demand remains high, despite the lack of scientific evidence that they actually do any good.

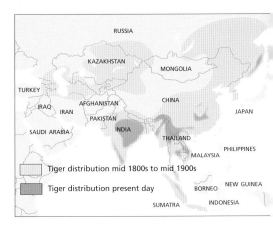

Tiger distribution mid 1800s to mid 1900s

Tiger distribution present day

Man-Eaters

Tigers are among the few animals known to frequently prey on people. Some tigers even seem to prefer human flesh over that of other species. Sometimes tiger predation has taken a huge toll on human life. For example, over 1,000 people a year were killed in Singapore in the 1940s, 1,000 a year in India in the 1970s, and even now about 100 a year in the Sundarbans mangrove forest near Calcutta. However, these alarming statistics actually relate to comparatively few tigers. Tigers are not born man-eaters; but it seems that once they have made a kill (perhaps after an accidental encounter), some realize the potential of the alternative food source and then exploit it. After all, an unarmed human cannot run fast and is relatively easy to kill. However, most tigers are wary of people and under normal circumstances will avoid any contact. Problem tigers are most common in places where human activity has encroached on their habitat, reducing the availability of natural prey and introducing alternatives such as domestic animals and people themselves.

flattened, and can separate the bones in a victim's spine with ease. A larger animal is more of a challenge; but once it is on the ground, a tiger kills it with a long, suffocating bite around the throat. Even when mortally wounded, a large animal like a gaur could kill a tiger with its flailing hooves, so the tiger maintains the throat bite long after the animal stops struggling, just to be sure it is really dead. It then drags the carcass under some kind of cover before feeding. An adult tiger can eat over 90 pounds (40 kg) of meat in one meal, but with a large kill the tiger is more likely to eat smaller quantities at intervals over the next few days. Sometimes several tigers are seen feeding from one carcass, but they are usually members of the same family.

Necessary Requirements

Although the tiger can live in a variety of habitats, it is restricted to environments that meet three vital requirements: There must be plenty of suitable prey, enough dense cover to allow the tiger to approach prey, and a reliable source of water. Areas of suitable habitat must also be large if they are to support a viable population of tigers. As a general rule tigers live alone, and animals of the same sex tend not to occupy the same range. The size of home ranges varies greatly from place to place, with males in Nepal typically claiming 8 to 40 square miles (20 to 100 sq. km). Male Siberian tigers, on the other hand, may range over 1,600 square miles (4,000 sq. km). Females occupy

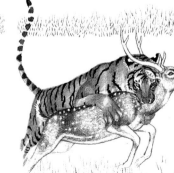

↧ *A tiger needs to attack prey from quite close range. It usually rushes a victim from behind, aiming its claws for the shoulder, back, or neck.*

↥ *A leaping Bengal tiger. Tigers have long hind limbs that enable them to leap up to 30 feet (10 m) in a single bound, helping them bring down prey.*

much smaller ranges; typically three or four females live within the range of one male, and he can mate with them all.

Tigers tend not to defend territories fiercely, and fights over land are unusual. Nonresident animals seem to respect the owner's rights. Although they may pass through each other's ranges, they do not stay long and keep out of the way. Resident tigers, especially males, visit all parts of their range regularly, leaving scent marks on trees and other landmarks. The marks not only let other tigers know the area is occupied, they also carry information about the individual that made them, such as its sex and reproductive condition. Scent marks fade; and if they are not

replaced within three or four weeks, another tiger may attempt to move in. In the case of males this usually means the original resident has died, although females may lose distant parts of their range while they are confined to a small area by the birth of their cubs.

⊕ *A white Bengal tiger. All white tigers in captivity are descendants of a white male captured in India in 1951.*

White Tigers

There is a rare variety of tiger that lacks the pigment which gives other tigers their characteristic orange coat. The dark stripes are still there, but the coat is otherwise creamy-white. Likewise, the tiger's eyes lack brown pigments and are pale blue. Not surprisingly, such animals have always been considered very special, so much so that they have apparently been eliminated from the wild by hunters and collectors. The last record of a wild white tiger was in 1958. Since then, however, many white specimens have been bred in captivity, and there are currently about 40 in zoos around the world.

Fighting is rare among tigers, but those spats that do occur are more often than not between females with cubs and unfamiliar males. Rearing cubs is the sole responsibility of the females, who are ferocious in defense of their young; a spirited attack may be enough to drive even a large male away. When a male takes over a new range, he will often attempt to kill any young cubs in the area. This is so that the females come into breeding condition sooner, and he can begin fathering offspring of his own. Young tigers are vulnerable for a long time: Fewer than half of all cubs live to more than two years of age, and infanticide (killing of young by adults) is by far the most significant cause of death. Once a male is established in an area and can be confident that all cubs are his own, his murderous tendencies subside, and he rarely makes any attempt to approach families.

Playful Cubs

A female tiger will choose a secure den, such as a cave or dense thicket, to give birth. The young stay there for up to two months while their mother leaves them for short periods in order to feed. After that the cubs emerge from the den; but they do not wander far, and their mother still returns at regular intervals to suckle them. Most of their waking lives are spent playing, building up the strength, agility, and coordination they will later use to deadly effect. By the age of five or six months the family begins to accompany their mother to hunt. By 11 months they are capable of catching and killing smaller prey items. Even so, they will still depend on their mother for at least part of their food until they are 18 months old and often remain under her protection for a further year. After that they move on, usually joining the ranks of nonbreeding, largely nomadic tigers that occupy marginal habitats on the fringes of occupied ranges, awaiting an opportunity to claim a range of their own.

⊖ *Licking cubs with the tiger's rough, hairy tongue helps keep them clean. Young tigers leave their mother, or may be pushed out, at the time her next litter is due.*

Common name Cheetah

Scientific name *Acinonyx jubatus*

Family	Felidae
Order	Carnivora

Size Length head/body: 44–59 in (112–150 cm); tail length: 24–31 in (60–80 cm); height at shoulder: 26–37 in (67–94 cm)

Weight 46–159 lb (21–72 kg)

Key features Very slender, long-limbed cat with small head, rounded ears, and long tail held in low sweep; fur pale gold to tawny, paler on belly with black spots; end of tail has dark bands

Habits Diurnal; can be solitary and nomadic or live in small groups

Breeding Litters of 1–8 (usually 3–5) cubs born at any time of year after gestation period of 90–95 days. Weaned at 3–6 months; sexually mature at 18 months but rarely breeds before 2 years. May live up to 19 years in captivity, up to 14 in the wild, but usually many fewer

Voice Purrs, yelps, moans, and snarls; also a high-pitched churring; females use birdlike chirping to reassure young

Diet Mostly gazelles and impalas; other hoofed animals depending on opportunity

Habitat Savanna grassland, scrub, and semidesert

Distribution Widespread but scattered populations throughout sub-Saharan Africa, excluding the Congo Basin. Small population in Iran

Status Population: fewer than 15,000; IUCN Vulnerable; CITES I. Range and population greatly reduced, now protected in most of its range

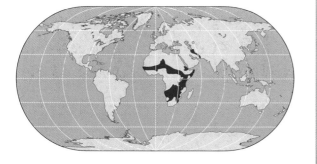

Cheetah

Acinonyx jubatus

Built for speed, the cheetah is the world's fastest land animal. However, its extraordinary sprinting ability is no defense against habitat loss and other pressures that threaten its existence.

THE CHEETAH IS THE FASTEST animal on four legs. Over even ground it can reach speeds of 65 miles per hour (105 km/h), and it has powers of acceleration that rival many modern sports cars. Its body is long and lean, like that of a greyhound, and its spine is remarkably flexible, allowing it to take huge strides that carry it forward up to 26 feet (8 m) in one bound.

Unrivaled Sprinter

The cheetah's legs are long but very slender, the lightness of the bones reducing the need for huge muscles. The paws are small but hard, with blunt, nonretractile claws that help it turn very fast. No other mammal has such extreme adaptations to speed, and none comes close to the cheetah in terms of sprinting ability. The fastest greyhounds, honed by centuries of selective breeding, reach about 40 miles per hour (65 km/h) over short distances. The American pronghorn antelope can run fast for longer distances, but cannot match the cheetah for acceleration and sprints.

The cheetah has made sacrifices for its supreme speed. Compared with other big cats, it has little stamina. In spite of the enlarged lungs and heart that keep oxygen circulating as fast as possible to the cheetah's muscles, it cannot keep up a full pursuit for more than about a minute. Three in every four hunts fail because the cheetah cannot get close enough to the prey before launching an attack.

The cheetah is not particularly powerful, and its relatively small teeth and claws do not make good weapons. The teeth have to be small in order to make room for the enlarged nostrils that enable the animal to breathe efficiently when running and when strangling

⊕ *A cheetah's power of acceleration and sprinting ability are unmatched by any other mammal. However, it begins to tire after 30 seconds and after a minute has virtually no chance of making a kill.*

its prey with a vicelike throat hold. But once the prey is dead, the cheetah has to spend a few minutes getting its breath back before dragging the prey to a secure place as fast as possible. If a scavenger spots the carcass, all the cheetah's efforts may have been for nothing, since it will rarely defend a kill against lions or hyenas. Cheetahs can even be scared off by vultures, although this may have more to do with the fact that vultures attract other, larger scavengers than a fear of the birds themselves.

Wasted Energy

If forced to abandon its hard-earned meal, a cheetah has to chase and kill again, using up yet more energy to feed itself. Being disturbed and driven off its food is a constant threat. Even in national parks where they are safe from other dangers, cheetahs are often forced by tourist buses to abandon their prey to scavengers.

Cheetahs do not seem to target old, young, or sick prey like other large carnivores, nor do they try to approach downwind. They simply select the animal that is nearest them or

one that is separate from the main herd and then try to outrun it. Mothers with cubs have a particularly hard time. They need to kill a gazelle or impala almost every day to keep their families well fed (compared with one every two to five days when there are no cubs). Before the age of three months, when they begin to gain some hunting sense of their own, the cubs can be a serious hindrance.

⊕ An adult cheetah stands among tall savanna grasses in Zimbabwe, southern-central Africa. Scattered cheetah populations are found throughout sub-Saharan Africa.

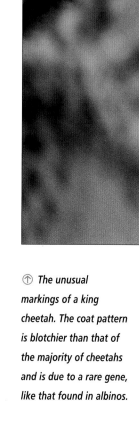

A cheetah suffocates a gazelle in Kenya. The animal's enlarged nostrils allow it to breathe efficiently while keeping a vicelike hold on its victim's throat.

Solitary Females

Female cheetahs are generally solitary. Unusually among cats, they have much larger home ranges than males, anything from 20 to 580 square miles (50 to 1,500 sq. km). They cannot hope to defend an area this size, and the ranges of several females usually overlap, although they rarely meet.

Males, on the other hand, are highly territorial, but unlike females rarely live alone. Territories are in such demand that the males have to team up in order to defend one. Such teams are known as coalitions and often contain two or three males, usually brothers. By working together, they can keep other males off their patch and win access to any females that might pass through. Cheetahs are not generally aggressive animals, but males from different coalitions have been known to fight to the death over females and territory. Fights within a coalition are very rare.

A pair of cheetahs may mate several times over a couple of days, but then they go their separate ways. The female gives birth in a secluded spot, usually in dense vegetation. The cubs are blind and helpless at birth, and the mother goes to great lengths to keep them hidden. She will move them one by one to a new hiding place if she suspects they have been spotted. After five weeks, however, they are able to follow her around.

For the first three months young cheetahs have a cape of long gray fur covering the back of the head, the shoulders, and back. It helps disguise their outline in long grass. Despite their camouflage and the mother cheetah's best efforts, the great majority of cheetah cubs do not survive to independence. Estimates of infant and juvenile mortality vary from 70 to 95 percent. A great many are killed by lions and hyenas, while many others starve or succumb to disease or congenital birth defects.

Threatened Existence

Cheetahs need open country with patches of tall grass or other vegetation, which they can use as cover when ambushing prey. However, much of this type of habitat has been given over to agriculture, depriving cheetahs of places to live. Hunting also took a grave toll on cheetah numbers in the past and remains a serious problem in some places.

Cheetah populations have undergone a worrying decline in recent years, despite legal protection for the species almost everywhere. At one time the species was widespread throughout Africa, the Middle East, and

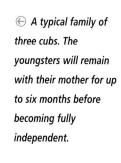

The unusual markings of a king cheetah. The coat pattern is blotchier than that of the majority of cheetahs and is due to a rare gene, like that found in albinos.

A typical family of three cubs. The youngsters will remain with their mother for up to six months before becoming fully independent.

southern Asia. Now there is only one population left outside Africa. It consists of a mere 250 animals and is found in northern Iran. In Africa the cheetah's distribution is now highly fragmented, and the small remaining populations are in danger of becoming inbred.

Studies of cheetah genetics have shown that there is very little individual variation. It seems that at some point in the past the cheetah population must have been extremely small. Today's population is therefore already rather inbred, with all the animals being virtually identical genetically. Now that populations are declining again, there are concerns that their lack of genetic variation could make the whole population vulnerable to disease or other natural disasters to which there will be no inherited resistance.

King Cheetahs

In 1927 zoologists studying cheetahs in Zimbabwe came to the conclusion that there were in fact two species in the area. The second, which they called *Acinonyx rex*, the king cheetah, was distinguished by a much blotchier coat pattern and a "mane" of longer hair around its shoulders. King cheetahs have always been rare, and until recently it was thought that they only occurred in Zimbabwe. However, a wild specimen has since been found on the edge of the Sahara in Burkina Faso, and a number of animals with king cheetah markings have been born in captivity. We now know that king cheetahs are not a separate species or even subspecies of cheetah. They are simply a rare genetic form of *A. jubatus* that turn up in the population, like albinos in other animals. King cheetahs can be born to normal-looking parents and have normal-looking siblings.

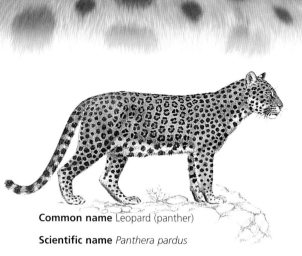

Common name Leopard (panther)

Scientific name *Panthera pardus*

Family	Felidae
Order	Carnivora

Size Length head/body: 35–75 in (90–190 cm); tail length: 23–43 in (58–110 cm); height at shoulder: 18–31 in (45–78 cm)

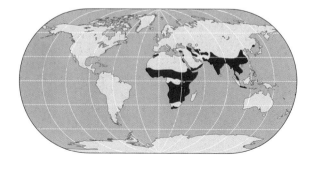

Weight Male 160–200 lb (73–90 kg); female 62–132 lb (28–60 kg)

Key features Large, lean cat with long tail; pale gold to tawny coat marked all over with black spots arranged into rosettes on back and flanks

Habits Solitary; mostly nocturnal; excellent climber

Breeding Litters of 1–6 (usually 2 or 3) young born after gestation period of 90–105 days during favorable season (varies throughout range). Weaned at 3 months; sexually mature at 3 years. May live over 20 years in captivity, probably well over 20 in the wild

Voice Rasping calls, grunts, and roars

Diet Mostly small- to medium-sized hoofed mammals; also monkeys, rabbits, rodents, and invertebrates, such as beetles

Habitat Varied; includes lowland forest, grassland, brush, and semidesert

Distribution Most of southern Asia and sub-Saharan Africa, excluding rain forests of Congo Basin. Small populations in North Africa, Middle East, Arabia, and China

Status Population: fewer than 700,000; IUCN Endangered and Critically Endangered (several subspecies); CITES I. Widespread but declining due to habitat loss and hunting

Leopard

Panthera pardus

The leopard is perhaps the archetypal big cat. It can still be found across wide areas of Africa and Asia, but some subspecies are now severely threatened.

THE LEOPARD'S NAME LITERALLY means "lion-panther," with panther or "pard" being the ancient general term for any large cat. Black or "melanistic" leopards, which are common in the forests of Southeast Asia, are still known as black panthers, but so are melanistic jaguars and pumas from the Americas.

Leopards have the largest geographical range of any species of the family Felidae except for the domestic cat. The leopard's range has shrunk over recent centuries, but its decline has not been nearly as precipitous as for other big cats such as the tiger. It still occurs widely in most of sub-Saharan Africa and southern Asia, with a few scattered populations in North Africa and the Middle East. Leopards are more tolerant of people than other large cats and manage to make a living in disrupted habitats that defeat many smaller predators.

Versatile Eating Habits

A large part of the leopard's success is due to its broad diet. It will eat almost any small- to medium-sized animal that it can catch, from an inch-long beetle to a 2,000 pound (900 kg) eland. In southern Africa the diet includes gazelles and impala, in the north wild pigs, in Asia mostly goats and sheep. The leopards in Israel eat rock hyraxes and porcupines, while Arabian leopards eat ibexes, partridges, and the occasional camel. Long-term studies have revealed that at least 90 species are regularly taken as prey, compared with just 12 normally taken by lions. Such versatility means that leopards can live in a wide variety of habitats and avoid direct competition with more specialized predators. Leopards can live almost

⬆ *Leopards are the best climbers of all the big cats and will spend time eating, resting, and sleeping in the branches of a favorite tree. They will even attack prey from tree branches, dropping down onto a victim from above.*

anywhere that provides sufficient cover and food, and they will modify their behavior to take advantage of the most abundant local prey. In some places this means hunting by day instead of night; elsewhere it has caused leopards to attack livestock and even humans.

Tree Dwellers

Of all the big cats, the leopard is the best climber. Its shoulders are especially muscular and provide most of the power necessary to pull it and its prey (often weighing twice as much as the leopard itself) into a tree. Caching (storing) food off the ground keeps it out of reach of most scavengers and gives the leopard the opportunity to feed at leisure. The leopard sleeps and eats in the branches and can descend headfirst, using flexible ankle joints and powerful claws to grip the treetrunk. There will be several favorite trees within a leopard's home range, which the animal returns to time and again. Forest leopards may drop down from the trees onto prey animals passing beneath, but they do not generally lie in wait, and such attacks are opportunistic rather than deliberately planned.

Leopards from different parts of the species' range can be markedly different in size and appearance. The largest individuals live in the well-stocked parks and game reserves of southern Africa, such as Kruger National Park, where males weighing over 200 pounds (90 kg) have been recorded. Elsewhere, leopards are much smaller, with those living in Arabia rarely exceeding 80 pounds (35 kg). Variations in coat color and pattern were used to split the species into dozens of subspecies. Many of them have been reassessed, and there are now about nine officially recognized subspecies based on geographical distinctions as much as on anatomical differences.

⊖ *A common color variation is the melanistic or black leopard. Such animals are often called "black panthers," but so too are black pumas and jaguars.*

During the 1960s over 50,000 leopards were killed every year to satisfy the demand for fashionable fur coats and stoles. Many populations were reduced to critically low levels: The leopard is now listed on Appendix I of CITES, so trade in skins and other parts is restricted and tightly controlled. Killing leopards for sport, however, is still permitted in several African countries where they remain relatively common. Today the demand for skins has been replaced by an increasing demand for body parts for use in traditional Asian medicines, and poaching is a serious problem for some of the more threatened subspecies. The leopard's wide distribution and the varying fortunes of its different subspecies mean that the subspecies are listed separately by the IUCN to draw attention to their status. Separate designations are useful to governments and other organizations trying to incorporate leopard conservation into plans for the development of some of the world's poorer countries, and they help strengthen the case for legal protection.

Home Ranges

Female leopards live in large home ranges, which may overlap at the edges. However, within the range there is always a core area that remains private. Such an area will have a reliable source of prey. It will also contain several trees or other secure places that are suitable for feeding, resting, and for hiding young. Male ranges are significantly larger. They overlap with those of up to six females to whom the male may have exclusive access for breeding. In spite of such a complex mosaic of leopard activity areas, the core of an individual leopard's home is usually respected, and strangers tend to keep away. Overlying male and female home ranges, there may be a third layer of less well-defined ranges occupied by younger, nonbreeding animals. Copious scent marking and vocalizations mean that unrelated leopards hardly ever meet.

Pregnant females do not build a nest, but will give birth to their cubs in a secure part of their core range. They may use a rocky crevice

Vulnerable to Attack

Unlike other members of the genus *Panthera*, which have no natural enemies other than humans, the leopard is vulnerable to attack and harassment by other predators. Young leopards are frequently killed by lions, hyenas, and wild dogs, and even fully mature adults will avoid confrontation with these species. Leopards have been known to abandon freshly killed prey when challenged by a single jackal or domestic terrier—animals less than half their size, which under other circumstances they might easily kill and eat. Females with young to feed and defend are more likely to stand their ground, but on the whole the leopard is strangely reluctant to fight or engage in a standoff that might attract yet more unwanted attention. Apparently, it is simply easier for the leopard to give up its prize and begin hunting again elsewhere.

⟲ *A snarling leopard. Despite its ferocious appearance it seems that the leopard is vulnerable to attack by other large predators. It will often choose to give up its prey rather than engage in confrontation.*

⟱ *A leopard with her cub of three months. Male cubs generally remain with their mother for 18 months, until they learn to hunt successfully. Daughters stay for longer, usually until the mother breeds again.*

or ledge as a den, or perhaps a tree hole or thicket of dense vegetation. High branches that make good resting places for an adult leopard would be much too dangerous for the cubs, which are born blind and barely able to crawl. Young leopards spend a long time with their mother. Unless the babies die very young, it will be at least two years before the female breeds again. Young males disperse first and go farthest away, so reducing the risk of inbreeding later on. Their mother will become less tolerant of them as soon as they learn to hunt successfully, usually at about 18 months. Daughters may stay close to their mother much longer and continue to share kills until the next family arrives. After that the younger females have little or no contact with their mother, although they may set up home nearby.

Common name Snow leopard (ounce)

Scientific name *Uncia uncia*

Family	Felidae
Order	Carnivora
Size	Length head/body: 39–51 in (100–130 cm); tail length: 31–39 in (80–100 cm); height at shoulder: 24 in (60 cm)

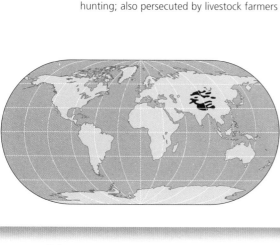

Weight Male 100–121 lb (45–55 kg); female 77–88 lb (35–40 kg)

Key features	Long-bodied cat with relatively short legs, small head, and long tail; fur is thick and pale gray to creamy-white, with gray spots and rosettes all over body, except the underside
Habits	Active dusk to dawn; solitary; very agile
Breeding	Litters of 1–5 (usually 2 or 3) cubs born April–June after gestation period of 90–103 days. Weaned at 2–3 months; sexually mature at 2 years. May live up to 15 years in captivity, 21 in the wild
Voice	Soft growls, grunts, and huffing sounds; moans loudly in courtship; does not roar
Diet	Mountain animals, including goats, deer, pikas, and marmots; some domestic animals
Habitat	Rocky mountainsides and grassy alpine plateaus at 9,000–20,000 ft (2,700–6,000 m)
Distribution	Mountainous parts of China, Nepal, Bhutan, India, Pakistan, Afghanistan, Uzbekistan, Tajikistan, Kazakhstan, Russia, and Mongolia
Status	Population: fewer than 7,000; IUCN Endangered; CITES I. In decline as a result of hunting; also persecuted by livestock farmers

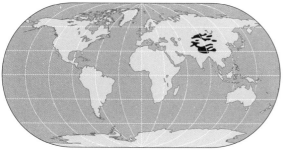

Snow Leopard

Uncia uncia

A large leopard of the high mountains, the snow leopard is a unique species. Although still widely distributed, it is now becoming scarce.

THE RARE AND BEAUTIFUL SNOW LEOPARD was once classified in the genus *Panthera* alongside big cats like lions and leopards. But unlike other big cats, the snow leopard cannot roar, and its characteristic postures and feeding technique are more like those of the smaller cats. In fact, it also resembles the small cats of the *Felis*, *Puma*, and *Lynx* genera is many other ways. For this reason zoologists have now placed the species in a genus of its own, called *Uncia*.

Thickly Furred Coat

Whatever its exact relationship with other members of the cat family, the snow leopard is undoubtedly one of the most attractive and enigmatic of all mammals. Its much coveted coat grows up to 3 inches (8 cm) thick and has a dense, woolly underlayer to protect the leopard from the bitterly cold weather in its mountain home. The fur even covers the soles of its huge feet, providing insulation against the icy ground and protection from sharp rocks. It also helps spread the cat's weight so that it can move over the surface of soft snow without sinking in. For an animal that spends most of its life above the snow line, it might be thought that a pure-white coat like a polar bear's would provide the best camouflage. But on the mountainsides of the Himalayas and Hindu Kush there are nearly always exposed gray rocks and stones, and against this type of background a snow leopard's highly patterned coat is virtually invisible.

The snow leopard has other adaptations to the cold, including large nostrils in which air is warmed as it is inhaled and cooled again on the way out. Exhaling warm breath into cold air wastes energy; it also creates puffs of condensation that could alert a prey animal to the leopard's presence, and it also could turn to ice on the cat's face. The fur on the face and head is not as thick as elsewhere; so when the snow leopard is sleeping, it curls its tail around as a muffler to keep its nose warm. The tail is extremely long and serves as a counterbalance when the leopard leaps from rock to rock.

⊕ Living on "the roof of the world," the rare and beautiful snow leopard has attained almost mythical status. Its wailing mating cries could be mistaken for those of a yeti.

Agile Hunter

Despite the chunky appearance created by the snow leopard's thick fur, it is one of the most agile members of the cat family. It is able to leap a vertical distance of about 20 feet (6 m) and is said to be able to travel 50 feet (15 m) in a single bound! This great leaping prowess is an important part of the leopard's hunting technique. So long as it can get close enough to prey like the Himalayan blue sheep, it can bring the animal to the ground and inflict a killing bite in one powerful movement. Large prey are eaten in several sittings over a period of a few days, after which the leopard moves on to a new hunting ground within its range.

Snow leopards occupy overlapping home ranges, but they are generally solitary. The size of the range depends on the local abundance of prey. In Nepal, for example, a leopard may spend most of its life in an area of little more than 5 square miles (12 sq. km). In Mongolia, on the other hand, a range may extend to over 400 square miles (1,000 sq. km) and include large expanses of desert plateau in between mountains.

Snow leopards are suffering greatly from loss of habitat to grazing livestock, and they are often persecuted as pests. Not surprisingly, their fur is highly sought after and even today can be found on open sale in some parts of Asia, despite legal protection. There are probably no more than 7,000 snow leopards left in the wild, and an intensive program of education and law enforcement is required throughout its range if the species is to survive.

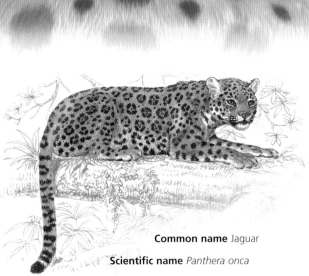

Common name Jaguar

Scientific name *Panthera onca*

Family	Felidae
Order	Carnivora
Size	Length head/body: 44–73 in (112–185 cm); tail length: 18–30 in (45–75 cm); height at shoulder: 27–30 in (68–76 cm)
Weight	Male 200–264 lb (90–120 kg); female 130–200 lb (60–90 kg)

Key features Large, robust-looking cat with short, thick tail and broad, heavy-looking head; fur pale gold to reddish-brown with spots arranged in rosettes and rings; black individuals known

Habits Solitary; territorial; active at any time of day but mostly around dawn and dusk; excellent swimmer and climber

Breeding Litters of 1–4 cubs born at any time of year in tropics after gestation period of 93–105 days (seasonal in north and south). Weaned at 5–6 months; sexually mature at 2–4 years. May live up to 22 years in captivity, 24 in the wild

Voice Grunts and mews

Diet Mostly peccaries and capybaras; also tapirs and other mammals; crocodiles and fish

Habitat Forests, scrub, grasslands, and semidesert; prefers habitats with water nearby

Distribution Central and South America south to northern Argentina and Paraguay

Status Population: unknown, probably several thousand; IUCN Lower Risk: near threatened; CITES I. Declining in range and population

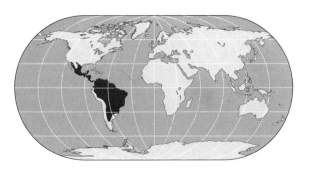

Jaguar

Panthera onca

The jaguar is the Western Hemisphere equivalent of the leopard, occurring widely in Central and southern America.

THE JAGUAR HAS A DISTINCTLY stocky build and short tail compared with its cousin the leopard. It is the largest cat in the Americas, having survived the mass extinction of other large mammals at the end of the Pleistocene era (2 million years ago). It managed to survive by preying on fish and large reptiles, such as crocodiles and turtles, and its massive jaws may have evolved as an adaptation for cracking open turtle and tortoise shells. This explains the jaguar's enduring fondness for waterside habitats; even though much of its prey is nowadays caught on dry land, it still kills by piercing the skull rather than by breaking the neck or strangulation the way other cats normally do.

From Hunter to Hunted

The arrival of European settlers and their livestock in the region probably provided an unexpected boost to the jaguar population in the form of several new species of potential prey. There is evidence that the new feeding opportunities actually increased jaguar numbers for a time. However, this period of growth was short-lived, since people began to hunt jaguars for skins and to protect themselves and their animals from attack. The trade in jaguar skins peaked during the 1960s, when tens of thousands of pelts were exported to Europe and the United States each year. Jaguars rarely attack people, but they will follow unwanted intruders, giving frightened humans the impression they are being stalked.

The range of the jaguar used to extend well into the southern United States, and the animal was once the dominant predator from Florida to Arizona. The last jaguars resident in the United States were probably eliminated quite early in the 20th century. However, wandering animals still occasionally cross the border from Mexico,

⊕ *Jaguars survived extinction 2 million years ago by preying on fish and reptiles. Today they catch most of their prey on land, but still prefer waterside habitats.*

and in 1996 there were two confirmed sightings in Arizona. But the Mexican population is declining, too, and may number fewer than 500 animals. Elsewhere, the jaguar is doing better, especially now that international law prohibits trade in its skins.

Territorial

Jaguars are territorial, but part of their home range can overlap with that of another individual. Male home ranges are at least twice as large as those occupied by females—up to 160 square miles (about 400 sq. km). Like tigers, male jaguars hold territories by prior right, thereby avoiding the need to fight over land. As long as the male continues to mark out his range, its boundaries will be respected by other males in the area.

Both sexes occasionally leave their range and wander widely, in many cases settling somewhere new. Such journeys may be associated with the movements of prey. Females that wander usually do so when they are ready to breed and may mate with several males along the way. It may be the only way a female can influence which male fathers her offspring, since an adult male can occupy the same range throughout his reproductive life.

↑ *Entirely black jaguars are relatively common. They are not a different species, but simply a genetically determined color variant.*

Common name Bobcat

Scientific name *Lynx rufus*

Family   Felidae

Order   Carnivora

Size   Length head/body: 25.5–41 in (65–105 cm); tail length: 4–7.5 in (11–19 cm); height at shoulder: 17.5–23 in (45–58 cm)

Weight 9–33 lb (4–15 kg)

Key features Small, slender-limbed, short-tailed cat; fur thick, varies in color from buff to brown with darker spots and streaks; ears pointed, often with tufts; ruff of fur around jowls

Habits   Solitary; territorial; active day or night

Breeding   Litters of 1–6 kittens born after gestation period of 60–70 days, usually in spring. Weaned at 2 months; females sexually mature at 1 year, males at 2 years. May live up to 32 years in captivity, probably no more than 13 in the wild

Voice   Usually silent, but hisses and shrieks in distress and during courtship

Diet   Small mammals and birds; sometimes larger prey, such as small deer; domestic animals

Habitat   Varied; includes forests, scrub, swamp, mountains, and the edges of deserts

Distribution North America

Status   Population: 700,000–1 million; CITES II. Declined in the past due to persecution; still harvested for fur under license in some states

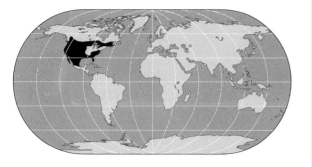

Bobcat

Lynx rufus

Territorial and solitary, the bobcat is sometimes confused with its close cousin, the lynx. Both cats have tufted ears and short tails, but the bobcat tends to be the more aggressive of the two.

THE BOBCAT IS SO CALLED because of its short tail, which resembles the docked bobtails of some domestic mammals. It looks a lot like another North American cat, the lynx, but there are few places where the two species live alongside each other. Bobcats are more aggressive than lynx and usually drive the latter out of habitats that suit both. However, the lynx is much better adapted to snow than the bobcat, which has small feet that sink in easily. So the northern limit of the bobcat's distribution is determined largely by the average snowfall.

Adaptable Cats

Bobcats are true generalists, which means they can live in almost any habitat; hence their wide natural distribution throughout most of North America. They are only absent where large areas are intensively cultivated or given over to industrial development. They are scarce in places where they have been overhunted. Their varied diet is a major factor in their adaptability. Their preferred prey appears to be rabbits and hares, but they will eat other small mammals and many larger ones too, including beavers, peccaries, and deer. Hoofed mammals are the main winter prey of bobcats in the north of their range, and Canadian bobcats are usually larger than those living in the south. This helps them cope with bigger prey.

The bobcat's hunting technique almost always relies on surprise. With its mottled coat providing admirable camouflage, a bobcat can sneak up on the most alert of victims, using a combination of stealth and endless patience. The kill is made with a sudden leap and a quick bite to the back of the neck, separating the backbones and severing the spinal cord.

Bobcats can be active at any time of day, but most animals adjust their activity to match that of their preferred prey. They wander up to 9 miles (15 km) a day in search of food, stopping often to mark and re-mark the boundaries of their home range. Females have smaller ranges than males—0.4 to 8 square miles (1 to 20 sq. km)—but they do not overlap with any others. Male territories can be anything from 2 to 16 square miles (5 to 40 sq. km), and they can overlap the ranges of other males and several females.

Respecter of Boundaries

Outside the breeding season bobcats go out of their way to avoid meeting, which leads to intensive scent marking to warn others away. Marks are made with urine and feces, and with secretions from the cat's anal glands. The marking is very effective, and bobcats appear to respect each other's territorial boundaries. Aggressive encounters seem very rare, and the ownership of a particular range area only changes when the resident animal dies.

⊕ Bobcats are solitary animals. Outside the breeding season they will go out of their way to avoid meeting and seem to respect each other's territories.

Of course, the need to breed means that males and females must meet at some point, and mating occurs any time between November and August. Most kittens are born in spring, but some births happen much later in the year. If a female loses her first litter of the year when the kittens are very young, she comes into season again and may produce a replacement litter in late summer. The kittens are able to follow their mother after three or four months, and they learn hunting skills by watching her. They stay with her until she is ready to breed again, then head off to find a place of their own.

There are probably about 1 million bobcats living in North America. They are protected in some states, notably those where the species has become rare. Elsewhere, they are hunted and trapped for part of the year, and their pelts sold to the fashion industry.

Common name Lynx (Eurasian lynx)

Scientific name *Lynx lynx*

Family	Felidae
Order	Carnivora
Size	Length head/body: 31–51 in (80–130 cm); tail length: 4–10 in (10–25 cm); height at shoulder: 23.5–29.5 in (60–75 cm)

Weight 18–84 lb (8–38 kg)

Key features Stocky cat with longish legs and large, furry feet; color varies from pale gray through yellow to reddish-brown; ears tufted

Habits Solitary; nocturnal; wanders widely

Breeding Litters of 1–4 kittens born April–June after gestation period of 67–74 days. Weaned at 3 months; females sexually mature at 9–21 months, males at 21–31 months. Lives up to 24 years in captivity, 17 in the wild

Voice Hisses and mews, but usually silent

Diet Mostly eats small- and medium-sized mammals, including hares and small deer

Habitat Mixed and taiga forest, scrub, steppe, rocky alpine slopes

Distribution Eurasian lynx: northeastern Europe, Balkans, Turkey, and the Middle East excluding Arabia, much of former U.S.S.R., Mongolia, and northern China. Iberian lynx: Spain, Portugal. Canadian lynx: Canada, Alaska, northern U.S.

Status Population: unknown, but certainly many thousands; IUCN Endangered (Iberian), Vulnerable (Canadian); CITES I (Iberian), II (Canadian and Eurasian). All have declined, mainly as a result of hunting for fur

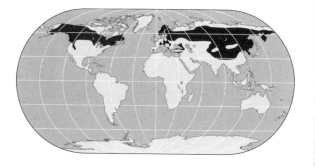

Lynx

Lynx lynx

A stocky, medium-sized cat, the lynx is widely distributed throughout the Northern Hemisphere. It is sometimes considered to be three separate species.

THERE IS AN ONGOING SCIENTIFIC debate about whether three of the recognized types of lynx are all members of the same species or not. The Canadian lynx (*L. canadensis*), Iberian lynx (*L. pardinus*), and Eurasian lynx (*L. lynx*) look remarkably similar, but they have different behavioral adaptations to suit life in their different parts of the world.

Distinctive Tail

Lynx are close cousins of bobcats (*L. rufus*), but can be told apart by examining the tail. Both species have short tails, but that of the lynx is completely black at the tip. In contrast, the bobcat's tail tip is black just on top. The largest lynx are Eurasian specimens from Siberia. They live on Arctic hares and other mammals several times bigger than themselves, such as reindeer (caribou). Snow can be an advantage to a hunting lynx, since deer can become bogged down and are then easier to catch. The lynx's feet are large and furry, so its weight is spread over a larger area, allowing it to run across snow without sinking. Iberian and Canadian lynx are about half the size of Eurasian lynx and generally hunt smaller prey.

Feeding Habits

The Canadian lynx feeds almost exclusively on snowshoe hares, and its numbers fluctuate from year to year according to the availability of the hares. Iberian lynx mainly feed on mammals such as rabbits, although they are also able to catch birds and fish, hooking them out of the air or water with a swipe of their sharp claws. For the smaller lynx a rabbit a day is sufficient food, but larger lynx eat rather more. Having killed a big animal such as a deer, they will drag it to safety, eat what they can, and cache (store)

⊕ *Snowy conditions can be advantageous for the hunting lynx, since its large, furry feet help spread its weight evenly and stop it from sinking into fresh snow. Lynx will often hunt deer that get bogged down in the snow and so are relatively easy to catch.*

the rest for later. Hunting is almost always a solitary activity, although mothers have sometimes been seen helping their fully grown young to hunt. Newly independent lynx sometimes team up with a sibling for the first few months after leaving their mother's care.

Endangered Species

Female lynx mature faster than males and can be capable of breeding within their first year. However, few do so because breeding is regulated by habitat availability. Lynx do not breed until they have found a suitable home range in which it will be possible to rear young. In places like Spain, where habitat is greatly restricted, adult lynx may never get the opportunity to breed. Of the few hundred Iberian lynx left in the wild fewer than a third are thought to be breeding females, making this one of the world's most endangered cats. Canadian and Eurasian lynx are faring better, although both have been extensively hunted in the past. Lynx fur is dense and luxurious, and several thousand animals are still legally shot or trapped every year for their fur.

In Central Europe lynx have been reintroduced to parts of Germany, Slovenia, and Switzerland; and while it is still early days for these cats, there are encouraging signs. The Swiss animals have bred successfully for several seasons, and some have now spread over the Alps into northern Italy of their own accord.

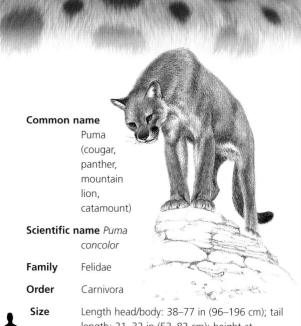

Common name
Puma
(cougar,
panther,
mountain
lion,
catamount)

Scientific name *Puma concolor*

Family Felidae

Order Carnivora

Size Length head/body: 38–77 in (96–196 cm); tail length: 21–32 in (53–82 cm); height at shoulder: 24–27.5 in (60–70 cm)

Weight Male 148–264 lb (67–120 kg); female 80–132 lb (36–60 kg)

Key features Large, muscular cat with long legs and tail; small head with large, rounded ears; coat color varies from silvery gray through warm buffy tones to dark tawny

Habits Solitary; active at any time of day; climbs extremely well

Breeding Litters of 1–6 (usually 3 or 4) kittens born January–June after gestation period of 90–96 days. Weaned at 3 months; sexually mature at 2.5–3 years. May live up to 21 years in captivity, rarely more than 14 in the wild

Voice Hisses, growls, whistles, and screams

Diet Carnivorous; mostly deer; also other hoofed animals, rodents, and hares

Habitat Very varied; lowland and mountain forests, swamps, grassland, and scrub

Distribution Most of North and South America

Status Population: many thousands in total, but Florida panther (*P. c. coryi*) fewer than 50; IUCN Critically Endangered (2 subspecies); CITES II (at least 2 subspecies). Persecuted as a pest in the past; now protected in parts of its range although still hunted in other areas

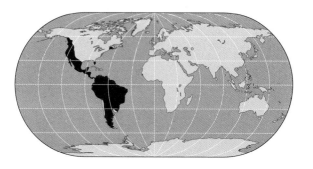

Puma

Puma concolor

The puma is the second largest cat in the Americas and by far the most widespread, with a natural range extending from Canada to Patagonia.

PUMA, COUGAR, PANTHER, AND MOUNTAIN lion are widely used names for the same animal—a highly adaptable, agile predator that feeds on medium-sized prey such as deer. Despite their larger size, pumas are more closely related to lynx and bobcats than to lions and jaguars, and are first cousins to the domestic cat. They are extremely agile and can climb with great ease. They prey mostly on ground-dwelling animals, but often use trees to lie in wait for passing animals, dropping on them from above. Alternatively, they may chase a prey animal for a short distance before leaping on its back. In either case the prey is killed with a bite to the neck. A lone adult puma may only need to kill every two weeks. It will drag the carcass to a safe place and hide it under a heap of dirt and debris, returning to feed on it again and again. For a mother puma with cubs life is rather more demanding, and she may have to kill a deer every three or four days to sustain her family.

Solitary Existence

Pumas are generally solitary, although young cats may stay with their mother for over a year and then remain together a few more months after she has left them. After the family disperses, young pumas live as nomads for a while, wandering through the ranges of resident pumas until they find a place to settle. While they may be capable of breeding by the age of two years, they will not do so until they have established themselves in a suitable home.

Females occupy large home ranges, which may overlap more or less completely with those of other pumas, but they avoid meeting by the use of scent marks and various vocalizations. Except when they have young kittens, females wander widely over their entire range, using

⊖ Pumas have a reputation for killing livestock such as sheep and cattle. In fact, they more frequently kill deer and tend to select old or weak individuals. In so doing they may be helping maintain a healthy deer population.

various patches of dense vegetation or small caves to rest in, rather than a regular den. Males operate in a similar way, except their ranges are much larger—sometimes over 400 square miles (1,000 sq. km)—and they overlap only with female pumas, not other males. They use scent marking more frequently than females, especially around the borders of their range. They do not generally fight over territory, and new residents only move in when the previous occupant dies.

Pumas have a reputation for killing livestock such as horses, cattle, and sheep, but that is relatively infrequent. They kill deer, too, but in so doing may actually help keep the deer population healthy, since they tend to select old or weak individuals. It also prevents the deer from getting too numerous. Pumas have been implicated in a number of fatal attacks on humans, but in general they avoid people.

Gradual Comeback

Intensive eradication attempts all but exterminated pumas from much of North America, leaving only small populations in the western mountains, southern Texas, and Florida. The animals appear to be making a gradual comeback in some Midwestern and eastern states, but they are still hunted in Texas. The Florida population is thought to number no more than 50 individuals, despite millions of dollars being spent on their conservation.

Common name Ocelot

Scientific name *Leopardus pardalis*

Family	Felidae
Order	Carnivora
Size	Length head/body: 22–39 in (55–100 cm); tail length: 12–18 in (30–45 cm); height at shoulder: up to 20 in (50 cm)

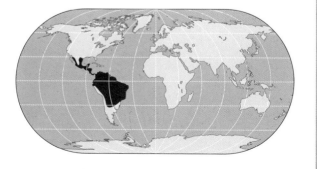

Weight 25–35 lb (11.5–16 kg)

Key features Pale gray to reddish or tawny cat, with variable pattern of dark spots and streaks around blotches of intermediate color; usually has dark tail rings and 2 cheek stripes

Habits Solitary; nocturnal; can climb and swim well but spends most of time on the ground

Breeding Litters of 1–3 kittens born at any time of year after gestation period of 79–85 days. Weaned at 6 weeks; females sexually mature at 18–22 months, males at 30 months. May live up to 21 years in captivity, 15 in the wild

Voice Yowls and meows like domestic cat

Diet Mainly rodents and rabbits, but known to catch small deer, monkeys, and wild pigs; also birds, reptiles, amphibians, and fish

Habitat Varied; includes tropical forest, swamp, mountainous areas, and dry scrub

Distribution Southwestern Texas, Central and South America down to northern Argentina

Status Population: 1.5–3 million; IUCN Endangered (Texas subspecies); CITES I. Possibly recovering in places, but Texas subspecies may number fewer than 100 animals, with only 150 in Mexico

Ocelot

Leopardus pardalis

Ocelot numbers are now recovering from heavy losses caused by hunting and trapping. The animal's beautiful, lustrous fur was highly prized at a time when wearing fur was considered fashionable.

IN THE 1960S AND 1970S THE exquisitely patterned coat of the ocelot was a common sight on the fashionable streets of Paris, around racecourses in England, and in the chic restaurants of Berlin and New York. Unfortunately, the coats were being worn by people, not cats. Ocelot fur was so sought after that over 200,000 wild animals were killed every year to supply the demand, more than any other cat. Most of the dead animals were exported from South and Central America to Europe, where by the 1980s an ocelot fur coat could fetch in excess of $800,000. Ocelots are not small animals, but it can take a lot of them to make just one coat because the furrier has to find pieces of fur whose patterns match along the seams.

New Problems

Hunting almost drove the ocelot to extinction in many places, but the species is now widely protected. In some parts of its former range it appears to be on the increase. In other areas ocelots are facing new problems, mostly involving loss of habitat. Ocelots are highly adaptable cats. They eat almost any small- to medium-sized animal and live in habitats as varied as tropical forest, thorny scrub, and mountains. Their only consistent requirement is that the habitat includes some dense vegetation in which to hide during the day. In the states of Texas and Louisiana such thickets have become very rare. Most have been grubbed out for agriculture or lost due to grazing by cattle. The ocelots that once lived there have all but disappeared. It is believed that there may now only be about 100 wild Texas ocelots left in the United States, restricted to the extreme southwest of Texas.

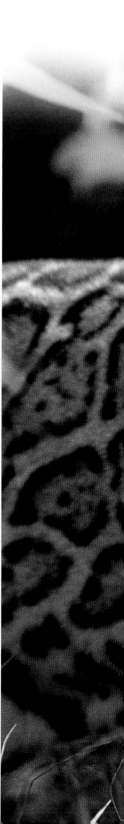

Intensive Research

The plight of the ocelot has prompted a program of intensive research into the species. As a result, it is now better known than many other small cats. Studies of ocelots in the wild have shown that while most animals live solitary lives, they manage to maintain social ties with their neighbors.

Female ocelots occupy a private home range of up to 4.5 square miles (11 sq. km). Males have ranges of up to twice the size,

⬇ *The ocelot's striking coat provides effective camouflage among the dense vegetation of the rain forest—but at one time made it a target for fur hunters and trappers.*

which overlap with those of several females. Males and females meet to breed, but apart from that are rarely seen together. Raising the family is very much the female's responsibility. In the tropics seasonal changes in the availability of food are insignificant, so ocelots can breed at any time of year. In the north of the species' range, however, they mate in winter, so the kittens are born in spring when there is plenty of prey to support them.

There are usually just one or two kittens, rarely three, but they are extremely lively and demanding. It is often as much as their mother can do to keep her small family out of danger as they try to investigate their world. Infant mortality can be high, and adolescents are much more prone to misadventure than experienced adults. All this means that the overall rate of population increase is frustratingly slow, even where the ocelot receives special protection.

Common name Serval

Scientific name *Caracal serval*

Family Felidae

Order Carnivora

Size Length head/body: 26–39 in (67–100 cm); tail length: 9–18 in (24–45 cm); height at shoulder: 21–24.5 in (54–62 cm)

Weight 20–40 lb (9–18 kg)

Key features Slender, long-limbed cat with longish neck and very large, rounded ears; coat is light beige to dark gold, pale on underside, and marked with variable black spots and streaks; black rings on tail

Habits Active by day or night; solitary and territorial; performs leaps when hunting, displaying, and as a means of seeing over long grass

Breeding One or 2 litters of 1–4 kittens born each year after gestation period of 74 days. Weaned at 6 months; sexually mature at 2 years. May live up to 20 years in captivity, 13 in the wild

Voice Growls, purrs, and shrill, far-carrying calls

Diet Mostly mice; also small mammals and birds

Habitat Riverside grasslands and reed beds; savanna regions, mountain grasslands

Distribution Most of sub-Saharan Africa, excluding Congo Basin and large deserts such as the Namib, Karroo, and Kalahari. Small outlying population in Morocco

Status Population: abundant; IUCN Endangered (Morroccan subspecies); CITES II. Common, but declining due to hunting and habitat loss

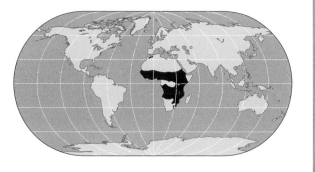

Serval

Caracal serval

Resembling a small, slender leopard, the serval occurs over most of Africa, except in deserts and dense forest.

THE SERVAL HAS BEEN DESCRIBED as the "cat of spare parts," and with its huge ears, small face, and elongated legs it is easy to see why. Early European explorers were obviously puzzled by this unlikely animal's behavior as well as its appearance—the name serval derives from the Portuguese words for "wolf-deer" and presumably refers to the serval's predatory nature and its deerlike leaps and bounds.

Most servals are marked all over with large black spots, but some have much finer markings, more like freckles. Animals like this are sometimes called servalines; they were once thought to be a different species. Now, however, we know that speckle-coated individuals are just a genetic variation and that both spotted and speckly kittens can occur in the same litter.

Graceful Hunters

Despite its gawky appearance, the serval is far from awkward. Its long legs and neck are an adaptation to life among tall grass and reed stems, and its enormous ears act as highly sensitive dish antennae, rotating this way and that to pinpoint the tiniest sound.

Servals are efficient hunters and succeed in making a kill in about half of their attempts. This success rate is even higher at night, but servals adjust their daily activity to the behavior of their preferred prey. For example, if most of the rats in an area are active by day, then the servals will be too. Ground-dwelling prey are located mainly by sound, then attacked with a typical catlike pounce. Servals can also catch birds, leaping up to 10 feet (3 m) out of the grass to swat them to the ground with their front paws. The serval's long legs can also be used for scooping small animals out of burrows, and the serval has flexible wrists and hooked claws to assist this action. If there is shallow

water nearby, the serval may wade in to hunt for fish or frogs.

Leaping Displays

Servals occupy fairly small home ranges, which overlap considerably. However, each animal has a core area of personal territory, which other servals usually avoid. Males are more territorial than females and may mark their core area with urine over 500 times a day. Intruding males are treated to a highly conspicuous display of bouncing and leaping, but disputes rarely become aggressive. Courtship is brief, since females are only receptive for a day at a time. The kittens are born in the long grass and moved regularly from place to place. Both adults and young are vulnerable to predation by hyenas, dogs, and leopards. Baby servals are

born with small ears, but they grow rapidly. The youngsters learn to hunt by watching their mother. She will drive the males of her litter away almost as soon as they can feed themselves, but young females stick around a bit longer. When they do leave, they will often set up home not far away.

Servals are widespread throughout sub-Saharan Africa and remain common in many parts of their range. Even so, they have still suffered their share of persecution and have been eradicated from populated areas, including most of South Africa. Serval fur is not especially valuable in itself, but pelts are used in traditional African costumes and sometimes sold to gullible tourists as baby leopard or cheetah skins. Some tribes regard serval meat as a delicacy.

⊙ The serval's alert, attentive appearance is indicative of its efficient hunting techniques. The huge ears can pinpoint the faintest sound.

Common name
Wildcat

Scientific name *Felis silvestris*

Family	Felidae
Order	Carnivora
Size	Length head/body: 20–30 in (50–76 cm); tail length: 8–14 in (21–35 cm); height at shoulder: 15–22 in (38–56 cm)

Weight 6.6–17.6 lb (3–8 kg)

Key features	Smallish cat with thick fur, very similar to a domestic tabby; tail noticeably bushy with blunt end
Habits	Solitary; mainly active between dusk and dawn; excellent climber
Breeding	Litters of 1–8 kittens born after gestation period of 61–68 days; births occur late spring in north, during rainy season in south, and year-round in tropics. Weaned at 30 days; sexually mature at 9–12 months. May live up to 15 years in captivity, fewer in the wild
Voice	Catlike mewing, hissing, and screeching
Diet	Mainly small mammals, especially rabbits and rodents; also birds, reptiles, and amphibians
Habitat	Forests, scrub, and open country with rocky crevices and patchy vegetation
Distribution	Scotland and southwestern Europe, including several Mediterranean islands; Africa (except for large deserts and tropical rain forests); Middle East and central and southern Asia, India, and north-central China
Status	Population: widespread and common; IUCN Vulnerable (Scottish population); CITES II (Scottish population). Globally abundant, but some local populations now very small

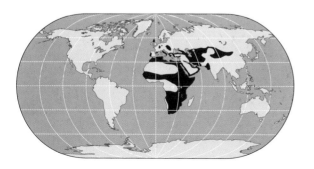

Wildcat

Felis silvestris

Wildcats are savage predators, yet one form has been domesticated for thousands of years and is much loved as a family pet the world over.

THE WILDCAT IS ONE OF THE most widespread members of the cat family, with a range extending from western Europe south to South Africa and east to India and China. Within its range, however, the species is split into many isolated populations, with some local variations in appearance, physiology, and behavior. European cats appear bigger than African cats because of their thicker coats, and gestation in European and central Asian cats is about a week longer than in their African cousins.

Nocturnal Predators

Wildcats live in a variety of habitats, but they do best where there are few people. They tend to be nocturnal and spend the day hiding in one of several dens within a home range of between 0.4 and 2 square miles (1 and 5 sq. km). In cooler climates they need to keep themselves warm in order to save energy. They will often spend time basking in the sun, either on the branch of a tree or on a secure rocky outcrop. By night they move around using regular pathways between favored hunting spots. They catch prey using a "stalk-and-pounce" technique. In Africa the diet is much the same all year round; in parts of Europe wildcats favor rabbits in spring when there are lots of babies to catch, and in the fall when the viral disease myxomatosis makes adults easy to attack. They also catch mice and voles, and often ambush birds feeding on the ground.

Males compete aggressively for the right to mate with a female, but then play no further part in raising their family. The young are born in a tree hollow or rock crevice where they depend on their mother's milk for the first month. After that they emerge from the den to play and follow their mother, who supplies

them with meat until they can catch their own prey. They disperse in the winter before the start of the breeding season, and some females may be mothers themselves before their first birthday. Males, however, rarely breed before they are two or three years old because of competition for females from older, more experienced cats.

Well-known Relative

The wildcat is the ancestor and closest relative of the domestic cat. The latter is thought to have appeared in Africa between 4 and 8 thousand years ago, a mere instant in evolutionary time. Sometimes the African wildcat is regarded as a separate species to other wildcats (yet still the origin of the domestic form). Other scientists consider wild and domestic cats to be the same species. It is certainly true that the two can interbreed successfully. In some parts of the wildcat's range so much hybridization is taking place that there may soon be no purebred wildcats left.

One of the most important differences between wildcats and their domestic relatives is temperament. True wildcats really are wild, elusive, and extremely ferocious. It is claimed they are impossible to tame. Indeed, they have every reason to detest humans. Studies of European wildcat populations show that up to 92 percent of all deaths are due to human interference, through hunting or persecution, accidental killing such as on roads, or in snares set for other animals. Wildcats are protected by law throughout Europe, but the expansion of human populations into previously unpopulated areas of wildcat habitat means they are unlikely to become common there ever again.

↩ *Wildcats are generally nocturnal and spend the day hiding in dens. In cooler climates they need to keep themselves warm and will often spend time basking in the sun on a tree branch or rock.*

The Hyena Family

Hyenas are dog-sized animals that are found throughout most of Africa. One species (the striped hyena) extends into Arabia and eastward to India. Typical hyenas get most of their food by scavenging and feed mainly on the kills of lions and other large carnivores. The animals have a reputation for being nasty. In fact, they are highly intelligent creatures, often with complex social behavior, and they play a vital role in clearing up the carcasses left by large predators.

What Is a Hyena?

Hyenas are doglike in appearance. They have weak hindquarters and back legs that are shorter than their forelegs. The shoulders are consequently higher than

their hips, and the head is carried low, giving the animals a distinctive hunchbacked appearance. The legs are long, and there is a large hairy tail. Typically, the coat color is sandy brown with dark stripes or spots. The jaws are powerful, and typical hyenas have massive crushing and shearing molar teeth for crunching up bones and tough bits of skin. Their digestive juices are so acidic they can digest bone fragments better than any other mammal. By contrast, the aardwolf hyena feeds on insects and has just 24 teeth (typical hyenas have 34). These teeth are small and reduced to simple, widely spaced pointed pegs.

Origins

Since few fossils are known to scientists, the origins of the hyena family are somewhat obscure. Hyenas may have evolved from a relative of the civets (family Viverridae) or an ancient type of mongoose (family Herpestidae). Alternatively, they may have had a separate evolutionary development, quite independent of the other families of carnivores.

Family Hyaenidae: 3 genera, 4 species	
Crocuta	1 species, spotted hyena (*C. crocuta*)
Hyaena	2 species, brown hyena (*H. brunnea*); striped hyena (*H. hyaena*)
Proteles	1 species, aardwolf (*P. cristata*)

⊕ *A pack of spotted hyenas gather around an elephant carcass. The animals gorge rapidly, consuming 25 to 30 pounds (11 to 14 kg) of flesh at a sitting. Group feeding is noisy, but rarely involves serious fighting.*

Hyenas are mainly nocturnal animals and prefer to rest during the day. However, some species—the spotted hyena for instance—may also be active in the daytime. The animals often shelter in dens among rocks and dense vegetation, sometimes using the abandoned burrows of warthogs or aardvarks.

Cooperative Hunting

Most hyenas live in clans of closely related individuals. Brown and striped hyenas tend to hunt alone, but spotted hyenas often cooperate to kill larger prey than they might otherwise manage. In some places about 90 percent of the spotted hyena's food consists of animals that it kills itself; elsewhere it is only half.

Spotted hyenas can chase their prey for over 2 miles (3 km), reaching speeds of more than 35 miles per hour (60 km/h). They can bring down animals as large as zebras, and soon a noisy pack gathers to grab at the victim, tearing off chunks and swallowing as fast as possible before going off to digest their hasty meals.

Cubs are born in a secure den, which is their operational base for up to 18 months. Spotted hyena cubs (usually twins) are born into a communal den shared with other pups of varying ages. Often there is squabbling among them,

and some pups may be killed as a result of aggressive interactions. Spotted hyenas are born with their teeth well developed. However, they are not fed on meat until they are nearly nine months old. Brown hyenas take meat to their cubs at a much earlier age, sometimes dragging large carcasses back to the den.

To some, the hyena's cringing appearance and weird calls are a sign of evil. Hyenas are often blamed for killing livestock and in the past were killed on sight. Today people are more tolerant, and no hyena species is seriously threatened. Hyenas are particularly common in national parks.

⬆ Brown hyena juveniles (above) play as an adult approaches with its kill.

⬅ The aardwolf (left) differs from other hyenas: It feeds on insects, lives in pairs rather than clans, and defends its territory against others of its species.

Striped Hyena Hyaena hyaena

Smaller in build than its close relative the spotted hyena, the striped hyena's behavior seems to be influenced by its larger, more gregarious cousin.

Common name Striped hyena

Scientific name *Hyaena hyaena*

Family Hyaenidae

Order Carnivora

Size Length head/body: 39–47 in (100–120 cm); tail length: 10–14 in (25–35 cm); height at shoulder: 26–30 in (66–75 cm)

Weight 55–119 lb (25–54 kg)

Key features A tall, slender hyena with thick neck, large eyes, and bold stripes; fur is long and shaggy with a high hairy crest extending down the middle of the neck and back; face and throat often black; tail white

Habits Solitary or lives in small clans of closely related individuals

Breeding One to 5 (usually 3) cubs born at any time of year after gestation period of 90 days. Weaned at 10 to 12 months; sexually mature at 2–3 years. May live up to 24 years in captivity, probably up to about 15 in the wild

Voice Generally quiet; occasionally growls or whines

Diet An omnivorous scavenger; takes small prey, but may kill larger animals; fruit and bones

Habitat Dry grassland and semidesert; also rocky hills

Distribution North and northeastern Africa; Middle East and Turkey east to India; up to 10,000 ft (3,000 m) in some mountainous areas

Status Population: relatively abundant. Has declined in numbers and distribution, but is still widespread and fairly numerous

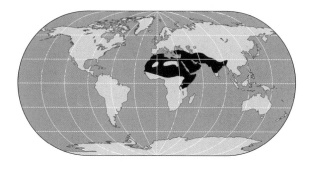

THE BEHAVIOR OF THE STRIPED HYENA tends to vary according to whether or not spotted hyenas are also present. Where the two species occur together, as they do in parts of northeastern Africa, the striped hyena tends to behave in a quiet and retiring manner and keeps a low profile. Elsewhere the species may be more prominent, sometimes living in large groups. In the northern parts of their geographical range striped hyenas may even hunt in small packs, just as the spotted hyena does farther south.

Clan Boundaries

Like other typical hyenas, the striped hyena sometimes lives in social groups called clans, which are made up of a number of closely related individuals. Each clan has a territory that is carefully marked out with scent produced from an anal pouch under the base of the tail. To deposit a scent marker (a process known as pasting), a hyena stands astride some stiff grass stems and wipes a patch of creamy-white paste onto the vegetation from the lips of its pouch. The process may also be used to mark rocks, shrubs, or pieces of dead wood. The clan will mark its territorial boundary with many thousands of pastings so that any intruding animals from a rival clan will know that they are trespassing. But the scent mark soon loses its smell and needs to be renewed, so members of the clan spend a lot of time patrolling their territory and pasting the grasses and shrubs.

Striped hyenas are sociable animals. When they meet, they erect the crest of long hair that runs down their back and sniff busily at each other. They make a particularly thorough inspection of the anal pouch, which may be turned inside out to assist the process. Close checking of each other's scent credentials not

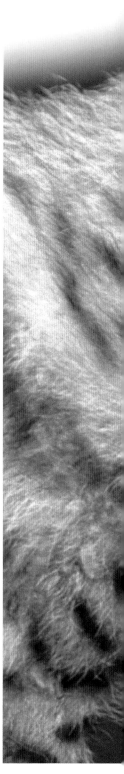

only helps hyenas ensure they belong to the same clan, but probably allows them to recognize each other as individuals. The smell will also convey information about sex, status, and breeding condition. Sometimes the greeting ceremony becomes rather lengthy and violent, especially between strangers. Initially it may involve gentle bites and mock fighting. But subordinate hyenas may be bitten quite hard, held by the throat, and shaken about. An angry hyena will arch its back and raise its hairs on end, often with its tail lifted, making it look much larger than normal.

Striped hyenas live in desert and rocky areas, a generally harsher environment than that enjoyed by the spotted hyena. Such habitat

⊖ *Striped hyenas are mainly scavengers and, unlike the spotted hyena, tend to forage alone. Since food can often be scarce in their desertlike habitat, the animals try to avoid competing with each other for food sources.*

Hair of the Hyena

The hairs on a striped hyena's mane and down the middle of its back are about 8 inches (20 cm) long, three times the length of the hairs on the rest of its body. An angry or excited hyena can make all its hair stand on end and bush out its tail. Standing high on its legs with its back arched, the animal may appear nearly 40 percent larger than usual. Often such an appearance is an effective form of intimidation and enables dominance to be established over subordinate animals without fighting or wasting extra energy.

extends across northern Africa and includes much of the Sahara Desert south to Tanzania, the Middle East as far north as Turkey, and eastward throughout most of India. Although striped hyenas inhabit dry areas, they tend to avoid true desert and make their homes where water is available for at least part of the year. Nevertheless, they can cope with very hot, dry conditions and avoid the heat of the day by being active mainly in the evening or at night. Midday is usually passed in the shade of overhanging rocks or among cool boulders. Some live in rocky areas, others in mountains up to nearly 10,000 feet (3,000 m), where temperatures may fall abruptly after dark.

Striped hyenas can also survive in very cold areas, provided they are also dry. Such bleak habitats often have little food to offer, so the hyenas are forced to range over extremely large areas. They can be found lying up in caves or shallow burrows, or among boulders. Some dens are used for long periods, especially when young are being raised.

Year-Round Breeding

Striped hyenas are capable of breeding from the age of two or three years and usually give birth to about three or four young, occasionally as many as five. Newborn infants weigh about 1.5 pounds (700 g). Striped hyena cubs are born blind, and their eyes do not open for about a week. Births can occur at any time of the year and follow a pregnancy period lasting 90 days. The young are fed on nutritious milk from their mother for the first month of life, after which they will come to rely increasingly on food brought to the den. Nonbreeding subadult animals from previous litters will often help feed the new members of the clan until they are able to fend for themselves, and it is not uncommon for large quantities of bones to accumulate at the entrance to the den.

The nursery den is usually a small collection of tunnels and chambers dug into the ground, but sometimes the animals will use rock crevices for a home. The cubs make a bleating call when they want attention or more food and

also when they become excited, especially during play. The nursery den is home to the cubs for up to a year before they become independent from their mother. It takes a long time for the young hyenas to find their way around and learn how to obtain food. Males leave their clan when they become mature and join another social group. It may take a while for the new male to be accepted by the group and to establish sufficient status to gain mating opportunities. Females normally stay with the clan that they were born into and eventually take on the status of their mother.

Threatening Behavior

As the young hyenas get older, their parents become increasingly intolerant of them. When offspring and parents meet, the greeting display needs to include ever more extended appeasement behavior on the part of the younger animals to avoid being attacked by their parents. Subordinate animals show their submissiveness by lowering the head, rolling their eyes, and sometimes lying down. Similar gestures are seen among domestic dogs confronted by dominant animals.

Aggression by dominant hyenas is accompanied by bristling the mane, extending the neck, and sometimes delivering a few sharp nips. Bites are usually aimed at the side of a hyena's neck where the skin is thick, so this kind of biting rarely results in serious wounds. Often minor fights occur, with the animals kneeling down. Fighting in such a way avoids the danger of getting the slender legs broken by an opponent's powerful jaws. Hyenas also threaten each other with growling noises that may rise to barks and be followed by snapping lunges at the opponent's neck.

Cleaning Up

Striped hyenas feed mainly on dead mammals. Food sources may be cattle, horses, or sheep that have died in the harsh, dry conditions. Alternatively, they may be the remains of prey killed by larger predators such as lions. Unlike spotted hyenas, striped hyenas do not benefit

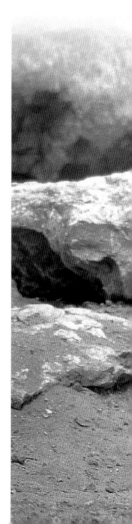

Striped hyena cubs live in dens for about a year—until they are independent from their mother. They survive on food brought to the den, often by nonbreeding older brothers and sisters.

from hunting in large clans. Even so, individual striped hyenas have been known to kill prey up to the size of an adult donkey. However, large mammals are usually too wary to be approached closely and also too strong to be easily killed. Hares, foxes, and large rodents are more common prey. The hyena's powerful jaws can easily cope with crunching up tortoises, grasshoppers, and occasionally smaller insects, such as termites.

Scavengers

Striped hyenas are more omnivorous than other species of their family and often eat wild and cultivated soft fruit and dates if they come across them. They will also eat birds and lizards. Under cover of darkness they often come to scavenge garbage dumps on the outskirts of human settlements. Surplus food may be stored in patches of dense vegetation. However, most of the time food tends to be scarce in the striped hyena's semidesert habitat, so the animals often forage alone to avoid competing with each other. They frequently range over areas of more than 20 square miles (50 sq. km), traveling 19 miles (30 km) in one

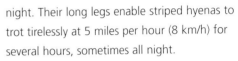

⤉ Striped hyenas check each other's scent credentials in elaborate greeting ceremonies. A meeting between strangers can involve bites and mock fighting or a throat hold in which a subordinate animal is roughly shaken.

night. Their long legs enable striped hyenas to trot tirelessly at 5 miles per hour (8 km/h) for several hours, sometimes all night.

There are reports of striped hyenas attacking and even killing people—especially children. Yet it is also reported that striped hyenas can become tame and affectionate pets. In some countries parts of the hyena's body are believed to have medicinal value, but in general, human attitudes toward hyenas tend to be rather negative. In North Africa and Arabia, for example, the striped hyena is regarded as a disgusting animal and widely suspected of being a grave robber. It is also unpopular in Israel because of the damage it does to crops of melons, grapes, cucumbers, and other succulent plants that provide moisture as well as food during dry weather. The animals are shot, poisoned, and trapped, but nevertheless manage to remain widespread and fairly abundant.

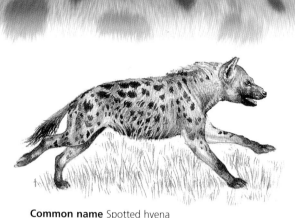

Common name Spotted hyena

Scientific name *Crocuta crocuta*

Family	Hyaenidae
Order	Carnivora
Size	Length head/body: 39–71 in (100–180 cm); tail length: 10–14 in (25–36 cm); height at shoulder: 28–35 in (70–90 cm)

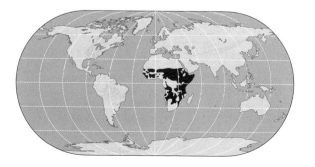

Weight 88–200 lb (40–91 kg); female generally about 12% heavier than male

Key features Doglike, powerfully built animal with short tail and sloping back; pale sandy gray coat with dark, irregular blotches

Habits Usually nocturnal, but will venture out during the daytime; lives in clans

Breeding Usually 2, but up to 4 cubs born after gestation period of 4 months. Weaned at 8–18 months; sexually mature at 2 years. May live to over 40 years in captivity, probably fewer in the wild

Voice Loud whooping noises; crazy-sounding giggle

Diet Meat from carcasses killed by other predators; slow animals like waterbuck; also tortoises, fish, insects, and garbage

Habitat Acacia savannas; urban fringes

Distribution Africa south of Sahara, except for areas of thick forest; absent from most of South Africa

Status Population: several thousand; IUCN Lower Risk: conservation dependent. Widespread and fairly common, but disappearing from many places being unpopular with farmers

Spotted Hyena *Crocuta crocuta*

The spotted hyena has few friends. It is rapidly disappearing from large parts of Africa as a result of its reputation as a killer and undesirable neighbor.

SPOTTED HYENAS LIVE IN SOCIAL groups called clans, which defend a shared territory against rival groups. The clan territory—which may be very large—is staked out with scent marks on logs and boulders. Clans may divide into smaller subgroups and live in a series of burrows that they dig for themselves. Bigger groups occupy a large communal den, often among rocks. Some dens have been used by generations of hyenas over hundreds of years. Although a clan may number over 40 animals, its members seem able to recognize each other, mainly by smell.

Big-Game Hunt

Hyenas are active mainly in the evening and early part of the night. A clan may gang together to kill large mammals such as a wildebeest or zebra. During a chase hyenas are known to manage speeds of 35 miles per hour (60 km/h) or more, but they soon tire and usually give up after less than a mile or so. Only about one-third of such hunts are successful.

Large victims are torn apart, with each hyena greedily swallowing as much as possible in a short time, often as much as 30 pounds (14 kg) of meat. Hyenas will take advantage of sick and injured animals and also pick at carcasses left by lions and other predators. Occasionally, larger groups of hyenas manage to force lions to abandon their fresh kills. Spotted hyenas are also known to exploit the large numbers of young wild antelope and zebra available during the calving season. They may even follow wildebeest herds to pester the females while they are giving birth.

However, most spotted hyenas live in small groups and prefer to forage alone. They may cover up to 50 miles (80 km) in a night, searching for whatever can be picked up with the least effort. Nowadays that often means garbage scavenged from around the edges of towns and villages, but hyenas will also eat reptiles, eggs, and even large beetles.

Breeding can occur at any time of the year, although only some females have offspring. In a communal den one female is dominant, but others in the same den may be allowed to breed. Young spotted hyenas are born blind and helpless, but develop fast. Only their mother feeds them, providing milk for up to 18 months. She does not normally carry food back to the den, and unlike some hyenas, other females in the clan do not assist in rearing the family. The dominant female is an overbearing individual, and others in the clan will allow her

Spotted hyenas are especially good at crunching up fresh bones using their massive jaws and teeth. The shearing teeth are extremely effective and can slice up tough sinews and thick mammal skin better than most knives.

to eat as much as she wants unchallenged. The general behavior of clan members centers around appeasing the dominant female. She will signal her aggressive mood by raising her tail and sometimes snarling. Unlike all other mammals, her sexual organs look almost exactly like those of a male.

Young hyenas are independent at about 12 to 16 months, and they are sexually mature at two years old. The females generally stay with the clan into which they were born, while the males disperse and join another clan, remaining there for a few years before moving on again. This ensures that the clans do not become inbred. There is no permanent bond between males and females.

Refuse Collectors

Formerly a successful and widespread species, the spotted hyena is still one of the most abundant large African carnivores. However, it has an uneasy relationship with people. Many believe that its weird laughing giggles and manic whoops are associated with evil spirits. Its cringing behavior and habit of scavenging around latrines and garbage dumps make the animal seem unclean. It is also known to attack and eat domestic stock. The spotted hyena has been shot and poisoned wherever land is taken for farming and has become quite rare over large parts of its former range. It is now only really abundant in protected areas such as national parks. Yet it has an important role to play, cleaning up after other animals. By scavenging, ripping apart carcasses, and crunching up bones, the hyena actually helps speed up decomposition.

Common name Aardwolf

Scientific name *Proteles cristata*

Family   Hyaenidae

Order   Carnivora

Size   Length head/body: 22–31 in
           (55–80 cm); tail length: 8–12 in
           (20–30 cm); height at shoulder:
           16–20 in (40–50 cm)

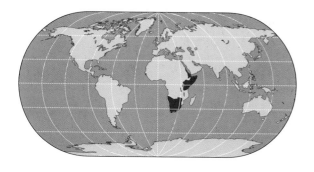

       Weight 18–26 lb (8–12 kg)

Key features Slender, creamy-brown animal with a few
           widely spaced black stripes; black feet,
           muzzle, and tail tip; coat often discolored by
           soil from den; molar teeth small and peglike

Habits   Nocturnal; territorial; normally forages alone

Breeding Two to 5 young born after gestation period
           of about 2–3 months. Weaned at 2–3
           months; sexually mature at 1 year. May live
           up to 20 years in captivity, fewer in the wild

Voice   Generally silent, but growls and barks when
           angry

Diet   Mainly termites; some other insects, including
           beetles and grasshoppers; occasionally mice

Habitat   Areas of dry, grazed grassland where termites
           are abundant

Distribution Southern Africa; separate subspecies in East
           Africa north to Eritrea

Status   Population: widespread, but generally scarce,
           although not seriously threatened

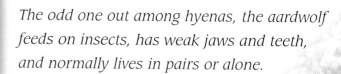

Aardwolf

Proteles cristata

The odd one out among hyenas, the aardwolf feeds on insects, has weak jaws and teeth, and normally lives in pairs or alone.

THE AARDWOLF IS A SPECIALIZED feeder, concentrating on termites. It seems to have evolved from an ancestral form of hyena, becoming different from the typical types about 20 million years ago. Unlike other termite-eating mammals, the aardwolf does not have powerful forelimbs or big claws with which to rip open or dig up termite nests. Instead, it takes harvester termites that normally forage on the surface rather than underground.

Termite Diet

The main food of the aardwolf is two types of termite, which tend to be active at different times of day. The preferred food is the snouted harvester termite, which cannot tolerate exposure to the sun and is therefore active only after dark. In winter or during the wet season they may be hard to find, so the aardwolf switches to another type of harvester termite that tends to be more active during the day.

    The availability of harvester termites is the main factor that governs where aardwolves live, and the relative proportions of the nocturnal and diurnal termites (those active by night and day respectively) dictate the activity patterns of the aardwolves themselves.

    Harvester termites swarm among dead grass, and aardwolves find them by constantly crisscrossing the ground and listening for the rustling of dry grass stems being invaded by the insect hordes and nibbled by thousands of jaws. The termites are lapped up with masses of sticky saliva. Since termites are only small insects, they do not need to be chewed much, and aardwolves have small, simple teeth (fewer than any other member of the hyena family). An aardwolf may consume nearly a quarter of a million termites in a single night.

⊕ The termite-eating aardwolf poses no threat to humans or livestock but has been persecuted along with other species of hyena. Yet despite such activities, aardwolf populations remain relatively stable.

Boundary Marking

Where termites are abundant, aardwolves can manage with smallish territories, sometimes less than 1 square mile (1 to 2 sq. km). Where food is scarce, on the other hand, territories are considerably larger. One territory may include over 3,000 termite nests containing more than 150 million termites. Since the nests are vital to the aardwolves, the animals guard their territories jealously. They mark the boundaries every 50 yards (40–50 m) or so, smearing grass stems with a smelly paste from glands under the tail. They chase off other aardwolves and also jackals, raising the stiff hairs along their back to make themselves look fiercer.

Aardwolves live alone or in pairs and may have up to 10 dens within their home territory. They breed seasonally, giving birth to between two and five cubs. Newborn cubs are helpless, but soon have their eyes open. They stay in the underground den for up to two months, guarded by their father, while the female forages. By the age of three months the cubs are feeding outside the den with one of their parents. They begin to disperse when they can fend for themselves. Before the parents' next family is ready to appear above ground, the cubs move off to find a feeding area of their own.

Aardwolves are harmless and pose no danger to people or livestock. Nevertheless, they have been persecuted along with other hyenas and also killed for their skins (used in tribal ceremonial rugs). In some areas they are at risk from insecticides used to kill locusts; and where termites are eradicated to allow farming, aardwolves cannot survive. Despite such problems, the aardwolf population remains relatively secure.

List of Species

The following lists all the carnivores in the families covered in this volume.

Order Carnivora (part)

FAMILY FELIDAE
Cat Family

Acinonyx

A. jubatus Cheetah; Africa, Middle East

Caracal

C. aurata African golden cat; Senegal to Democratic Republic of Congo and Kenya

C. caracal Caracal (lynx, African lynx); Africa and Asia from Turkestan and N.W. India to Arabia

C. serval Serval; Africa

Felis

F. bieti Chinese desert cat; C. Asia, W. China, S. Mongolia

F. chaus Jungle cat; Egypt to Indochina and Sri Lanka

F. margarita Sand cat; N. Africa, S.W. Asia

F. nigripes Black-footed cat; S. Africa, Botswana, Namibia

F. silvestris Wildcat; W. Europe to India; Africa (*F. s. catus* Domestic cat; worldwide, introduced by man)

Leopardus

L. colocolo Pampas cat; Ecuador to Patagonia

L. geoffroyi Geoffroy's cat (Geoffroy's ocelot); Bolivia to Patagonia

L. guigna Kodkod (Chilean cat, huiña); C. and S. Chile, W. Argentina

L. jabobita Mountain cat (Andean cat); S. Peru to N. Chile

L. pardalis Ocelot; Arizona to N. Argentina

L. tigrinus Tiger cat (little spotted cat, ocelot cat, oricilla); Costa Rica to N. Argentina

L. wiedii Margay cat (tigrillo); N. Mexico to N. Argentina

Lynx

L. canadensis Canadian lynx; Alaska, Canada, N. U.S.

L. lynx Lynx (Eurasian or northern lynx; W. Europe to Siberia

L. pardinus Iberian lynx; Spain and Portugal

L. rufus Bobcat (red lynx); S. Canada to S. Mexico

Neofelis

N. diardi Clouded leopard (island species); Sumatra and Borneo,

N. nebulosa Clouded leopard (mainland species); India, S. China, Nepal, Burma, Indochina, possibly also Taiwan (may be extinct)

Otocolobus

O. manul Pallas's cat (manul); Iran to W. China

Panthera

P. leo Lion; S. Sahara to S. Africa, excluding Congo rainforest belt; Gujarat, India (a remnant population in Gir Forest Sanctuary)

P. onca Jaguar; S.W. U.S. to C. Patagonia

P. pardus Leopard; Africa south of the Sahara, and S. Asia; scattered populations in N. Africa, Arabia, Far East

P. tigris Tiger; India, S.E. Asia; China; S.E. Russia

Pardofelis

P. badia Bay cat (Bornean red cat); Borneo

P. marmorata Marbled cat; Sumatra, Borneo; Malaya to Nepal

P. temmincki Asiatic golden cat (Temminck's golden cat); Nepal to S. China and Sumatra

Prionailurus

P. bengalensis Leopard cat (Bengal cat); Sumatra, Java, Borneo, Japan, Philippines, Taiwan

P. planiceps Flat-headed cat; Borneo, Sumatra, Malaya

P. rubiginosus Rusty-spotted cat; S. India and Sri Lanka

P. viverrinus Fishing cat; Sumatra, Java, to S. China and India

Puma

P. concolor Puma (cougar, mountain lion, panther); S. Canada to Patagonia

P. yaguarondo Jaguarundi (jaguarondi, eyra, otter-cat); Arizona to N. Argentina

Uncia

U. uncia Snow Leopard; C. Asia from the Himalayas to S. and W. Mongolia and S. Russia. Occurs in 12 countries, with China constituting 60 percent of its total range.

FAMILY HYAENIDAE
Hyena Family

Crocuta

C. crocuta Spotted hyena (laughing hyena); Sub-saharan Africa, except Congo rain forests and far south

Hyaena

H. brunnea Brown hyena (beach or strand wolf); widespread in S. Africa, particularly in the west; also into S. Angola

H. hyaena Striped hyena; N.W. and N.E. Africa, Syria, Asia Minor, Caucasus, India, Arabia

Proteles

P. cristata Aardwolf; S. Africa and E. Africa

Glossary

Words in SMALL CAPITALS refer to other entries in the glossary.

Adaptation features of an animal that adjust it to its environment; may be produced by evolution—e.g., camouflage coloration

Adaptive radiation when a group of closely related animals (e.g., members of a FAMILY) have evolved differences from each other so that they can survive in different NICHES

Adult a fully grown animal that has reached breeding age

Anal gland (anal sac) a gland opening by a short duct either just inside the anus or on either side of it

Antler branched prongs on the head of male deer, made of solid bone

Arboreal living among the branches of trees

Arthropod animals with a jointed outer skeleton, e.g., crabs and insects

Biodiversity a variety of SPECIES and the variation within them

Biomass the total weight of living material

Biped any animal that walks on two legs. See QUADRUPED

Breeding season the entire cycle of reproductive activity from courtship, pair formation (and often establishment of TERRITORY), through nesting to independence of young

Browsing feeding on leaves of trees and shrubs

Cache a hidden supply of food; also (verb) to hide food for future use

Callosities hardened, thickened areas on the skin (e.g., ischial callosities in some PRIMATES)

Canine (tooth) a sharp stabbing tooth usually longer than rest

Canopy continuous (closed) or broken (open) layer in forests produced by the intermingling of branches of trees

Capillaries tiny blood vessels that convey blood through organs from arteries to veins

Carnassial (teeth) opposing pair of teeth especially adapted to shear with a cutting (scissorlike) edge; in living mammals the arrangement is unique to Carnivora, and the teeth involved are the fourth upper PREMOLAR and first lower MOLAR

Carnivore meat-eating animal

Carrion dead animal matter used as a food source by scavengers

Cecum a blind sac in the digestive tract opening out from the junction between the small and large intestines. In herbivorous mammals it is often very large; it is the site of bacterial action on CELLULOSE. The end of the cecum is the appendix; in SPECIES with a reduced cecum the appendix may retain an antibacterial function

Cellulose the material that forms the cell walls of plants

Cementum hard material that coats the roots of mammalian teeth. In some SPECIES cementum is laid down in annual layers that, under a microscope, can be counted to estimate the age of individuals

Cheek teeth teeth lying behind the CANINES in mammals, consisting of PREMOLARS and MOLARS

CITES Convention on International Trade in Endangered Species. An agreement between nations that restricts international trade to permitted levels through licensing and administrative controls. Rare animals and plants are assigned to categories: (for example Appendix 1, 2). See Volume 1 page 17

Cloven hoof foot that is formed from two toes, each within a horny covering

Congenital condition an animal is born with

Coniferous forest evergreen forests of northern regions and mountainous areas dominated by pines, spruces, and cedars

Corm underground food storage bulb of certain plants

Crepuscular active in twilight

Cursorial adapted for running

Deciduous forest dominated by trees that lose their leaves in winter (or the dry season)

Deforestation the process of cutting down and removing trees for timber or to create open space for activities such as growing crops and grazing animals

Delayed implantation when the development of a fertilized egg is suspended for a variable period before it implants into the wall of the UTERUS and completes normal pregnancy. Births are thus delayed until a favorable time of year

Den a shelter, natural or constructed, used for sleeping, giving birth, and raising young; also (verb) the act of retiring to a DEN to give birth and raise young or for winter shelter

Dental formula a convention for summarizing the dental arrangement, in which the numbers of all types of tooth in each half of the upper and lower jaw are given. The numbers are always presented in the order: INCISOR (I), CANINE (C), PREMOLAR (P), MOLAR (M). The final figure is the total number of teeth to be found in the skull. A typical example for Carnivora is I3/3, C1/1, P4/4, M3/3 = 44

Dentition animal's set of teeth

Desert area of low rainfall dominated by specially adapted plants such as cacti

Diastema a space between the teeth, usually the INCISORS and CHEEK TEETH. It is typical of rodents and lagomorphs, although also found in UNGULATES

Digit a finger or toe

Digitigrade method of walking on the toes without the heel touching the ground. See PLANTIGRADE

Dispersal the scattering of young animals going to live away from where they were born and brought up

Display any relatively conspicuous pattern of behavior that conveys specific information to others, usually to members of the same SPECIES; can involve visual or vocal elements, as in threat, courtship, or greeting displays

Diurnal active during the day

DNA (deoxyribonucleic acid) the substance that makes up the main part of the chromosomes of all living things; contains the genetic code that is handed down from generation to generation

DNA analysis "genetic fingerprinting," a technique that allows scientists to see who is related to whom, for example, which male was the father of particular offspring

Domestication process of taming and breeding animals to provide help and useful products for humans

Dorsal relating to the back or spinal part of the body; usually the upper surface

Droppings see FECES and SCATS

Ecosystem a whole system in which plants, animals, and their environment interact

Edentate toothless, but is also used as group name for anteaters, sloths, and armadillos

Endemic found only in one small geographical area and nowhere else

Estrus the period when eggs are released from the female's ovaries, and she becomes available for successful mating. Estrous females are often referred to as "in heat" or as "RECEPTIVE" to males

Eutherian mammals that give birth to babies, not eggs, and rear them without using a pouch on the mother's belly

Extinction process of dying out in which every last individual dies, and the SPECIES is lost forever

Eyeshine where the eyes of animals (especially CARNIVORES) reflect a beam of light shone at them. This is caused by a special reflective layer (the tapetum) at the back of the eye;

characteristic of many NOCTURNAL species and associated with increased abilities to see in dark

Family technical term for a group of closely related GENERA and SPECIES that often also look quite similar. Zoological family names always end in "idae." Also used as the word for a social group within a species consisting of parents and their offspring

Feces remains of digested food expelled from the body as pellets. Often accompanied by SCENT secretions

Feral domestic animals that have gone wild and live independently of people

Flystrike where CARRION-feeding flies have laid their eggs on an animal

Fossorial adapted for digging and living in burrows or underground tunnels

Frugivore an animal that eats fruit as main part of the diet

Fur mass of hairs forming a continuous coat characteristic of mammals

Fused joined together

Gape wide-open mouth

Gene the basic unit of heredity enabling one generation to pass on characteristics to its offspring

Generalist an animal that is capable of a wide range of activities, not specialized

Genus a group of closely related SPECIES. The plural is genera

Gestation the period of pregnancy between fertilization of the egg and birth of the baby

Grazing feeding on grass

Gregarious living together in loose groups or herds

Harem a group of females living in the same TERRITORY and consorting with a single male

Herbivore an animal that eats plants (grazers and browsers are thus herbivores)

Heterodont DENTITION specialized into CANINES, INCISORS, and PREMOLARS, each type of tooth having a different function. See HOMODONT

Hibernation becoming inactive in winter, with lowered body temperature to save energy. Hibernation takes place in a special nest or DEN called a hibernaculum

Homeothermy maintenance of a high and constant body temperature by means of internal processes; also called "warm-blooded"

Home range the area that an animal uses in the course of its normal periods of activity. See TERRITORY

Homodont DENTITION in which the teeth are all similar in appearance and function

Horns a pair of sharp, unbranched prongs projecting from the head of CLOVEN-HOOFED animals. Horns have a bony core with a tough outer covering made of KERATIN like our fingernails

Hybrid offspring of two closely related SPECIES that can interbreed, but the hybrid is sterile and cannot produce offspring of its own

Inbreeding breeding among closely related animals (e.g., cousins) leading to weakened genetic composition and reduced survival rates

Incisor (teeth) simple pointed teeth at the front of the jaws used for nipping and snipping

Indigenous living naturally in a region; NATIVE (i.e., not an introduced SPECIES)

Insectivore animals that feed on insects and similar small prey. Also used as a group name for animals such as hedgehogs, shrews, and moles

Interbreeding breeding between animals of different SPECIES or varieties within a single FAMILY or strain; interbreeding can cause dilution of the gene pool

Interspecific between SPECIES

Intraspecific between individuals of the same SPECIES

Invertebrates animals that have no backbone (or other true bones) inside their body, e.g., mollusks, insects, jellyfish, and crabs

IUCN International Union for the Conservation of Nature, responsible for assigning animals and plants to internationally agreed categories of rarity. See table below

Juvenile a young animal that has not yet reached breeding age

Keratin tough, fibrous material that forms hairs, feathers, and protective plates on the skin of VERTEBRATE animals

Lactation process of producing milk in MAMMARY GLANDS for offspring

Larynx voice box where sounds are created

Latrine place where FECES are left regularly, often with SCENT added

Leptospirosis disease caused by leptospiral bacteria in kidneys and transmitted via urine

Mammary glands characteristic of mammals, glands for production of milk

Marine living in the sea

Matriarch senior female member of a social group

Metabolic rate the rate at which chemical activities occur within animals, including the exchange of gasses in respiration and the liberation of energy from food

Metabolism the chemical activities within animals that turn food into energy

Migration movement from one place to another and back again, usually seasonal

Molars large crushing teeth at the back of the mouth

Molt the process in which mammals shed hair, usually seasonal

Monogamous animals that have only one mate at a time

Montane in a mountain environment

Mustelid small CARNIVORE (e.g., weasel) belonging to the FAMILY Mustelidae

Mutation random changes in genetic material

IUCN CATEGORIES

EX	**Extinct**, when there is no reasonable doubt that the last individual of a species has died.	**VU**	**Vulnerable**, when a species faces a high risk of extinction in the wild in the medium-term future.
EW	**Extinct in the Wild**, when a species is known only to survive in captivity or as a naturalized population well outside the past range.	**NT**	**Near Threatened**, when it is not CR, EN or VU, but is close to qualifying for those categories
CR	**Critically Endangered**, when a species is facing an extremely high risk of extinction in the wild in the immediate future.	**LC**	**Least Concern**, when a species has been evaluated and does not satisfy the criteria for CR, EN, VU, or NT.
		DD	**Data Deficient**, when there is not enough information about a species to assess the risk of extinction.
EN	**Endangered**, when a species faces a very high risk of extinction in the wild in the near future.	**NE**	**Not Evaluated**, species that have not been assessed by the IUCN criteria.

Native belonging to that area or country, not introduced by human assistance

Natural selection when animals and plants are challenged by natural processes (including predation and bad weather) to ensure survival of the fittest

New World the Americas; OLD WORLD refers to the non-American continents (not usually Australia)

Niche part of a habitat occupied by an ORGANISM, defined in terms of all aspects of its lifestyle

Nocturnal active at night

Nomadic animals that have no fixed home, but wander continuously

Old World non-American continents. See NEW WORLD

Omnivore an animal that eats almost anything, meat or vegetable

Opportunistic taking advantage of every varied opportunity that arises; flexible behavior

Opposable fingers or toes that can be brought to bear against others on the same hand or foot in order to grip objects

Order a subdivision of a class of animals consisting of a series of related animal FAMILIES.

Organism any member of the animal or plant kingdom; a body that has life

Ovulation release of egg from the female's ovary prior to its fertilization

Pair bond behavior that keeps a male and a female together beyond the time it takes to mate; marriage is a "pair bond"

Parasite an animal or plant that lives on or within the body of another

Parturition process of giving birth

Pelage furry coat of a mammal

Pelt furry coat; often refers to skin removed from animal as fur

Pheromone SCENT produced by animals to enable others to find and recognize them

Physiology the processes and workings within plants and animal bodies, e.g., digestion. Maintaining a warm-blooded state is a part of mammal physiology

Placenta the structure that links an embryo to its mother during pregnancy, allowing exchange of chemicals between them

Plantigrade walking on the sole with the heels touching the ground. See DIGITIGRADE

Polygamous when animals have more than one mate in a single mating season. MONOGAMOUS animals have only a single mate

Polygynous when a male mates with several females in one BREEDING SEASON

Population a distinct group of animals of the same SPECIES or all the animals of that species

Posterior the hind end or behind another structure

Predator an animal that kills live prey for food

Prehensile grasping tail or fingers

Premolars teeth found in front of the MOLARS, but behind the CANINES

Pride social group of lions

Primate a group of mammals that includes monkeys, apes, and ourselves

Promiscuous mating often with many mates, not just one

Protein chemicals made up of amino acids. Essential in the diet of animals

Quadruped an animal that walks on all fours (a BIPED walks on two legs)

Range the total geographical area over which a SPECIES is distributed

Receptive when a female is ready to mate (in ESTRUS)

Reproduction the process of breeding, creating new offspring for the next generation

Retina light-sensitive layer at the back of the eye

Retractile capable of being withdrawn, as in the claws of typical cats, which can be folded back into the paws to protect them from damage when walking

Riparian living beside rivers and lakes

Roadkill animals killed by road traffic

Rumen a part of the complex stomach found in RUMINANTS specifically for digesting plant material

Ruminant animals that eat vegetation and later bring it back from the stomach to chew again ("chewing the cud" or "rumination") to assist its digestion by microbes in the stomach

Savanna tropical grasslands with scattered trees and low rainfall, usually in warm areas

Scats fecal pellets, especially of CARNIVORES. SCENT is often deposited with the pellets as territorial markers

Scent chemicals produced by animals to leave smell messages for others to find and interpret

Scrotum bag of skin within which the male testes are located

Scrub vegetation dominated by shrubs—woody plants usually with more than one stem

Secondary forest trees that have been planted or grown up on cleared ground

Siblings brothers and sisters

Social behavior interactions between individuals within the same SPECIES, e.g., courtship

Species a group of animals that look similar and can breed to produce fertile offspring

Spraint hunting term for SCATS (see above) of certain CARNIVORES, especially otters

Steppe open grassland in parts of the world where the climate is too harsh for trees to grow

Sub-Saharan all parts of Africa lying south of the Sahara Desert

Subspecies a locally distinct group of animals that differ slightly from the normal appearance of the SPECIES; often called a race

Symbiosis when two or more SPECIES live together for their mutual benefit more successfully than either could live on its own

Taxonomy the branch of biology concerned with classifying ORGANISMS into groups according to similarities in their structure, origins, or behavior. The categories, in order of increasing broadness, are: SPECIES, GENUS, FAMILY, ORDER, class, and phylum.

Terrestrial living on land

Territory defended space

Thermoregulation the maintenance of a relatively constant body temperature either by adjustments to METABOLISM or by moving between sunshine and shade

Translocation transferring members of a SPECIES from one location to another

Tundra open grassy or shrub-covered lands of the far north

Underfur fine hairs forming a dense, woolly mass close to the skin and underneath the outer coat of stiff hairs in mammals

Ungulate hoofed animals such as pigs, deer, cattle, and horses; mostly HERBIVORES

Uterus womb in which embryos of mammals develop

Ventral the belly or underneath of an animal (opposite of DORSAL)

Vertebrate animal with a backbone (e.g., fish, mammals, reptiles), usually with skeleton made of bones, but sometimes softer cartilage

Vibrissae sensory whiskers, usually on snout, but can be on areas such as elbows, tail, or eyebrows

Viviparous animals that give birth to active young rather than laying eggs

Vocalization making of sounds such as barking and croaking

Zoologist person who studies animals

Zoology the study of animals

Useful Websites

General

http://animaldiversity.ummz.umich.edu/
University of Michigan Museum of Zoology animal diversity websites. Search for pictures and information about animals by class, family, and common name. Includes glossary

http://www.cites.org/
IUCN and CITES listings. Search for animals by scientific name, order, family, genus, species, or common name. Location by country; explanation of reasons for listings

http://endangered.fws.gov
Information about threatened animals and plants from the U.S. Fish and Wildlife Service, the organization in charge of 94 million acres (38 million ha) of American wildlife refuges

http://www.iucn.org
Details of species and their status; listings by the International Union for the Conservation of Nature, also lists IUCN publications

http://www.nccnsw.org.au
Website for threatened Australian species

http://www.ewt.org.za
Website for threatened South African wildlife

http://www.panda.org
World Wide Fund for Nature (WWF), newsroom, press releases, government reports, campaigns

http://www.aza.org
American Zoo and Aquarium Association

http://www.ultimateungulate.com
Guide to world's hoofed mammals

http://www.wcs.org
Website of the Wildlife Conservation Society

http://www.nwf.org
Website of the National Wildlife Federation

http://www.nmnh.si.edu/msw/
www.nmnh.si.edu/msw/
Mammals list on Smithsonian Museum site

Specific to this volume

http://www.carnivoreconservation.org/
News, links, recent books, etc., on carnivore ecology and conservation

http://www.defenders.org/
Active conservation of carnivores, including wolves and grizzly bears

http://www.wwfcanada.org/en/res_links
/pdf/projdesc.pdf
Carnivore conservation in Rocky Mountains

http://www.5tigers.org
Comprehensive information about tigers

http://www.wildlifetrustofindia.org
Information about Indian wildlife, including tigers

Picture Credits